THE FULL MOUNTIE

AND OTHER HIGHLIGHTS FROM

THE GLOBE CHALLENGE

WARREN CLEMENTS

M&S

National Library of Canada Cataloguing in Publication

Clements, Warren, 1952-
    The full mountie and other highlights from the Globe Challenge / Warren Clements.

ISBN 0-7710-2155-0

    1. Canadian wit and humor (English)   2. Play on words.
I. Title.

PS8555.L435F84 2003   C818'.5402   C2003-901672-2
PR9199.3.C527F84 2003

We acknowledge the financial support of the Government of Canada through the Book Publishing Industry Development Program and that of the Government of Ontario through the Ontario Media Development Corporation's Ontario Book Initiative. We further acknowledge the support of the Canada Council for the Arts and the Ontario Arts Council for our publishing program.

Typeset in Minion by M&S, Toronto
Printed and bound in Canada

McClelland & Stewart Ltd.
The Canadian Publishers
481 University Avenue
Toronto, Ontario
M5G 2E9
www.mcclelland.com

1 2 3 4 5   07 06 05 04 03

To all the Globe and Mail *readers who put pen to paper, or fingers to keyboard, to make the Challenge possible.*

And to my mother Ann, my sister Rebecca, my nephew Anthony and my wife Sandra, for their love and support.

ACKNOWLEDGEMENTS

This book would not have been possible without the *Globe and Mail*'s decision to let the column begin, thrive, and, when it was threatened, return. My thanks to William Thorsell, who was editor-in-chief at the column's birth, and to current editor-in-chief Edward Greenspon and editorial-page editor Drew Fagan for their support and willingness to allow me the time to assemble this book. Thanks as well to editors and colleagues past and present for their assistance, including Sarah Murdoch, Joan Danard, Martin Levin, Jack Kirchhoff, Alison Gzowski, and Suzanne Buhasz. Brian Gable, Mike Kesterton, and Phil Jackman have lent an ear when it mattered, and offered much-appreciated counsel. Finally, I thank McClelland & Stewart, and in particular my editor, Alex Schultz, for enthusiastically shepherding this book into print.

Contents

INTRODUCTION

The question asked most often about the *Globe* Challenge is the most difficult to answer: Who is Alanna Little?

I know she lives in Toronto. Bits of correspondence over the years suggest she is married. She appears to live or work within toppling distance of the CN Tower. Her entries appear regularly in the *Globe and Mail*'s Challenge column – not weekly, as some insist, but more often than not. Although a few other entrants appear at least as often, something about her name leads readers to wonder what the deal is with this Alanna Little person. Some complain that she's always there, taking up space that might more profitably be used by, say, the person who is complaining. Others grow worried when her name hasn't appeared for a few weeks.

But I haven't investigated further, just as I haven't called up Barrie Collins in Courtenay, B.C., or asked Karl Dilcher in Halifax for a chat. It's difficult enough to do the judging in this contest without being accused of playing favourites or, worse, of penalizing people for appearing too often; so I have made it a rule not to seek out the regulars for conversation, much as I would love to. The company of the Challengentsia, as one reader dubbed them, must be scintillating, given the level of wit and ingenuity that goes into their entries.

Oh, right. The entries.

Every week the column pitches the ball to an unknown quantity of batters, and every week they return it with an unpredictable force and spin. Ask for sentences in which a crucial letter is dropped from a word and they supply "The barbers' union elected a new hairman" (Phil Gurski) or "With his new dentures, chewing teak became a great challenge" (Ken Purvis). Ask for lines that would abruptly end a book and they offer "Aye, Captain Ahab, we saw the great white whale, and we killed it" (Peter Marucci) or "Here's Waldo" (Pierre G. Gagnon) or "Thank heavens my sisters are going to the ball. Now I can catch up on my reading" (Michael Davies).

The Challenge first saw daylight on February 2, 1991. The *Globe and Mail* had been running a contest by that name, but it was, if you'll pardon the frankness, dreary. Readers were expected to fill in the blanks in a factual paragraph; the answer was either right or wrong. There was little in it to satisfy an imaginative player, and the *Globe* soon realized it. The column died.

Inspired by witty columns in *Books in Canada*, *The Spectator*, and elsewhere, I proposed a challenge that would tax readers' ingenuity. My appeal must have made quite an impression, because I didn't hear another word about it for several months. Happily, art director Tony Sutton one day realized he had a spot to fill in his layout for the Saturday Focus section and asked whether the space was large enough for the Challenge. Yes, yes, I said. And tentatively I laid out the brief for readers.

"Its purpose is to entice readers to write limericks, submit anagrams, compose parodies, chronicle brief lives, gild lilies and otherwise exercise their wits in the service of the Muse. A new Challenge would be set each Saturday. Rules will be stated briefly, and accompanied by an example. The entry deadline will be ten days later (a Tuesday), and the best of the bunch will be published that weekend, with authors duly credited."

The first week's Challenge was to compose a limerick based on a well-known Canadian individual in the news. The verses that ran on February 9 (an initial sampling) and February 16 (the final cull) were encouraging. The most memorable was by Frank O'Brien of Saint John, about environmentalist David Suzuki:

Suzuki has rare civic pride,
And litter he cannot abide.
His grounds are so neat
The birds wipe their feet
Before they dare enter inside.

A sore point from the beginning was the selection of the weekly winner. Invariably friends and strangers who read the column criticized my choice. They couldn't agree on who should have won, but they were baffled that I had passed up this or that gem in favour of so obvious a dud. I started turning for a second opinion to colleague Brian Gable, editorial cartoonist extraordinaire, who has often caused me to reconsider my initial instincts, and always for the better.

You may have noticed that in the paragraph at the top of page 2 there was no annotation of Ahab, Waldo or the woman with sisters. The assumption from the start has been that Challenge readers have a broad base of cultural knowledge and would prefer not to have the jokes spelled out, since half the fun comes from recognizing the allusions. You may miss one, but you'll catch the next. Sometimes a joke that needs explanation is good enough that the rule is bent, but it's an exception.

Any misstep in the column immediately draws informed and (usually gently) chastising letters. When the column asked for a short, elegant sentence containing all twenty-six letters of the alphabet, and used the example (suggested by a *Globe* colleague) "Pack my box with five dozen liquor jugs," J.S. Cameron wrote, "Warning! You appear to be plagiarizing Stephen Jay Gould's latest book, *Bully for Brontosaurus*, Page 73. 'Pack my box with five dozen liquor jugs' is right there as a pangram. He asks his readers to submit a perfect pangram – all 26 letters used only once and no proper names. I've sent him mine, which goes: 'Why flex? Viz, track jogs numb, PDQ.' (A perfect 26-er.)"

The space allotted to the column has shrunk, grown and wandered from page to page, though it has found a lovely home of late in the Saturday Books section and in recent years has occupied a

corner of cyberspace on the *Globe and Mail*'s Web site. David Dunsmuir wrote on January 20, 1992, "Did I miss an announcement about the deep-freezing – or deep-sixing – of my favourite contest? The Challenge doesn't seem to have appeared for the past two weekends." It had gravitated to the bottom right-hand corner of Page 4 of the Focus section, next to the gardening column. At times I thought of attaching a bell to the darned thing.

A dicier moment arrived in 1996, when my superiors decided the column had been around too long and told me to wrap it up gracefully. Arguments that it had played to the *Globe*'s strengths by tapping the imagination of a terrific assortment of writers went for naught. The column stopped on September 21, 1996.

Immediately there was a torrent of protests, some from contributors and most from other readers. Among them was a verse from Kurt Loeb:

Higgledy piggledy,
Globe and Mail Challenges
Brightened my Saturdays,
Sharpened my mind.
That part of life has gone
Unacademical.

Now I'll just stay in bed,
Leave thoughts behind.

Craig Swick wrote from Maryland: "I was fortunate enough to have some of my entries published. This obviously demonstrates that Challenge editor Warren Clements has good taste. There were of course other weeks when my entry was clearly much better than the ones printed. I had all kinds of theories about why these were picked, but finally I realized he wanted to give other people a chance."

Linda Lumsden offered reasons for the Challenge to continue. "You get to see your name in print in a way that is not associated with a court appearance, scandal or death." Also, "it helps the economy (sale of envelopes, stamps, fax machines, Internet time etc.)."

On November 9, the column returned, preceded by a paragraph in the front-page index: "The barrage of letters, calls, faxes and e-mail messages was unremitting. Okay, readers, you win. The Challenge returns tomorrow in Focus."

Has the column changed over the years? To some extent, yes. Although I set an anagram contest as early as March 2, 1991, and received such inspired entries as ROBERT STANFIELD: ORNATE BRIEFS LTD., from Garry Newton, and (finance minister) MICHAEL WILSON: WISH ALL INCOME, submitted by both Murray Munn and Sheila McGivern, I would not set one now. Internet sites exist that extract all possible anagrams from any phrase a user submits, which rather takes the fun out of it.

As bait for entries, the column offers a book to the weekly winner, on the order of a dictionary or thesaurus. This brought an amusing double-dactyl response from Alanna Little – remember her? – after one of her victories in one of the contests:

Higgledy piggledy
Challenge contributors
Say their reward is the

Mots they devise.
Now that I've got my new
Globe and Mail Style Book, I
Have to recant and say
No, it's the prize.

With respect, I'd say it's the entries. This book will help me win the argument.

NEAR-CLASSICS

Naming a book can fray the nerves. Will the title resonate with readers? Will it reflect the contents, and not steer them to the wrong section in the bookshop? Will it sell?

John O'Byrne, a regular correspondent from Dublin, wondered about those book titles that didn't quite make it: The Raisins of Wrath, or Jude the Obvious, or Goodbye Mr. Fries. He suggested in 1996 that readers come up with other examples, which they gleefully did. Every second reader offered Moby Richard, though Mary Ellen Salmon came up with Moby Ricardo and Cherry Watson submitted Mopy Dick. Saul Kaufman promptly ingratiated himself with me by referring to that week's prize as the Globe and Mail Book of How to Write Good.

John Wright, who proposed He and It (the first and third books of the H. Rider Haggard trilogy), also offered a few examples, such as Catch 1 through 21, in honour of one of comedian Victor Borge's stage routines. "You will recall that Victor Borge's uncle invented a soft drink called 1-Up. It did not sell. He changed the formula and called it 2-Up. Nothing. In quick succession, 3-Up, 4-Up, 5-Up and 6-Up went the same way. He died not knowing how close he came."

Henrietta Johnson bemoaned the fact that "in reviewing my library recently, I could not find these titles," which included Chicken Salad for the Soul and Romeo and Julietta Anna Teresa Maria

mopy dick

Caroline. *"They obviously did not quite make it. More's the pity. Some might have had interesting plots, but who are we to judge?"*

Edward S. Hrelec, who suggested Milton's first draft might have been Paradise Misplaced, *proposed a variation on the theme. He speculated that a few famous titles might be revised to make them more politically correct:* Snow White and the Seven Vertically Challenged Persons *and* The Posture-Challenged Person of Notre Dame.

Among the titles that didn't make it to the marketplace:

The Caine Letter-Writing Campaign   MARK HANSON

Prosciuttolet   CHARLES COOK

The Black-Velvet Painting of Dorian Gray   LUCAS REBICK

All Creatures of Various Sizes   S.F. SOMMERFELD

Men Are From Pukatawagen, Women Are From Gypsumville
          JAMES L. WALKER

The Stone Hasti-Notes   IRMA COUCILL

Ad Hockery

It is not widely known that the Challenge exists to give advertisers ideas. Every now and then the Challengentsia collectively sit down and reel off promotional gimmicks, startling slogans and captivating copy that would make any advertising agency worth its salt show up the next day with chequebook in hand. Hasn't happened yet, but the century is young.

In 1997, we went after the endorsements of dead celebrities and literary figures.

Charles Darwin, for Turtles chocolates: "Your natural
  selection."　　　　　　　　　　　　　　**GEORGINA DONALD**

Julius Caesar: "I came, I saw, by Concorde!"　　**GLEN ACORN**

E.M. Forster, for Sprint: "Only connect."　　**KEN PURVIS**

Hester Prynne, for Fidelity Mutual Funds: "They get an
  A-plus."　　　　　　　　　　　　　　　　**RON CHARACH**

Socrates, for Herbal Teas: "I'll bet you thought we were
  related, didn't you?"　　　　　　　　**GLENN PATTERSON**

Alanna Little, who had suggested the contest (*Hamlet for Vicks:* "*Ay, there's the rub*"), wrote: "*In any case, I think we should blame Eric Mendelsohn for starting this with his 'Hitch your wagon to a star' in the April 5 column.*" Mr. Mendelsohn had, in response to an earlier assignment to provide familiar maxims with contemporary translations, translated "*Hitch your wagon to a star*" as "*Celebrity endorsements make minivans glamorous.*"

Ms. Little, *whose attention to the Challenge often trumps my own, picked up on an intriguing coincidence. The* Globe and Mail *had just carried a photograph of a fellow whose kilt was blown revealingly upward by a gust of wind. A few days before that, Linda Lumsden had entered the challenge to suggest offbeat candidates for the title of the greatest or bravest man or woman who had ever lived – a challenge that ran the day after the photo appeared.* "*Everyone knows that the Challenge illuminates past and current events as well as future ones,*" Ms. Little wrote, "*but how did Linda Lumsden know when she commended 'the first man to wear a kilt' in No. 252 that the* Globe *would publish the 'Question Answered' Black Watch photo on April 25?*"

Around the same time, the assignment was to suggest small advertisements guaranteed to elicit no reply.

"Architect from Pisa looking for new skyscraper challenge."
CAROLYN HARVEY-SMITH

"Jackhammer practice area needed by apprentice. Call 555-1234."
JEANNE DENEE

"Looking for passenger to share expenses on cross-country drive from Halifax to Vancouver. Must like reptiles and polka music."
DAVE NILES

"Paintings for sale by Picaso, Gogan, Van Go, Dally, Suzanne and others."
BERT GASKELL

"Trainee knife-thrower needs new partner. Apply Box 1234."
PETER BRODIE

It was a small jump from there to suggesting advertisements that no one was likely to believe. "An odd challenge this week," wrote Peter Marucci. "It implies that people really believe what advertisements say in the first place." Nevertheless, the ads flooded in.

"New from Microsoft: The last piece of software you'll ever have to buy. Runs on any hardware. Never upgrade again!"
ALYSSA DIAMOND

"Buy Acme Brussels sprouts. They're delicious. Enjoyed by children everywhere."
ADRIAN CHADWICK

"Foolproof mousetrap: catches mice, not fingers. During critical tests of this device carried out by Gerald Ford, the ex-president received no injury to his person."
B.W. JACKSON

Not enough to get those ad agencies salivating? Then how about the time the assignment was to suggest slogans that would sell hard-to-sell products?

"Make mealtimes fun while sharpening your baby's sense of balance with the new Unstable High Chair, now with Extra Wobble!"
BRYAN CADDY

Car that won't start: "The ultimate in fuel economy."
AL WILKINSON

Week-old newspapers: "Avoid surprises! Read history in the making!"
GORDON FINDLAY

Goldfish cages: "Never change the water again."
PETER MARUCCI

Used cooking oil: "Flavour-added oil for the adventurous cook!"
PETER BARWIN

nd finally, why not rope those dead celebrities and fictional char-acters into opening their own businesses and then *dreaming up slogans?*

Beethoven's Internet Service: Dot-dot-dot-com.
Homer Simpson's bakery: Dough!!! JOHN HANNAH

Einstein Jams and Marmalades: Unifying field berries for
over half a century. R.T. SIMON

Picasso Comedy Club: Never a straight face. KEN PURVIS

Carter Candy Bar Co.: May contain peanuts. KEN O'BRIEN

Frankenstein Innovations: We bring ideas to life.
DOUG KOLB

Freud Rental Cars: We try harder – because we're compensating for a lack of parental affection dating back to childhood.   PAUL KOCAK

Churchill's Chimes: They strike the finest hours.
                                                    F.W. MORGAN

Bonnie and Clyde's Travel Inc.: Let us plan your next getaway.   LINDA ROBB

Pavlov's Conditioner: Your hair is guaranteed to respond perfectly every time.   COLIN EYSSEN

John McEnroe's Whine Bar: Don't complain about the service. We already have.   BRIAN YAMASHITA

CHANGE A LETTER

⬤ ne of the more popular Challenges was to change one letter of a familiar, non-English phrase and redefine it. In a few cases, readers would add a letter (that was another Challenge) instead of changing one, or would change two letters, and sometimes those entries would be side-splittingly funny. The pattern I followed was to disqualify them for the first go-round, but to include them if a second batch ran later. I particularly enjoyed Barbara Laskin's "Cogito, dim sum: I'm thinking of ordering Chinese food."

The mangling of foreign phrases is high on the list of found material that friends send to friends over the Internet. As far as I can tell, they crib their favourite answers from newspaper and magazine contests and ruthlessly remove the names of the authors. I can't count the number of times I have been sent a batch of responses that the Washington Post's *Style Invitational* ran years ago, the one in which *Frisbeetarianism* is defined as the belief that after you die, your soul goes up on the roof and gets stuck there. People keep rediscovering these sorts of things on the Net, being amused by them and sending them off to everyone on their mailing lists – but without a crumb of credit to the originators.

It is not unusual for many contributors to come up independently with the same entry. Alanna Little remarked upon the fact after she and another contestant had submitted the same joke about product endorsements. *(She lost the coin toss.)* "Once again I'm amazed that, no matter how bizarre the Challenge, you receive duplicate entries. It must give you rare insight into your contributors' minds, akin to profiling, handwriting or ink-blot analysis. What a shock."

In the case of this contest, at least four people submitted "L'état c'est Mom," defined as "Mother is in charge around here." There were even duplicate entries for "Dipso facto: Definitely drunk," which added a letter rather than changed it.

Here, duly annotated, are a few familiar non-English phrases with one letter changed. Peter Marucci wrote: "We don't have enough trouble getting answers in English – you've got to come up with foreign phrases?" R.W. Crosby wrote: "I was tempted to enter 'Weakly Challenge,' but realized that it failed to quite qualify as being a foreign phrase."

Après moi le deluxe: I'm just the prototype.

DICK & SUE WATERMAN

Cogito, argo sum: I think I am a football player.

PETER MARUCCI

Flit accompli: They escaped.

JIM PARR

flit accompli

Dieu et mon droid: I am programming my robot to pray.

PETER WARREN

Muchas grabias: He can't keep his hands to himself.
Veni, vidi, bici: I had to complain about the tape I rented.

DAVID DUNSMUIR

I pluribus unum: I have a multiple personality disorder.

HENRYK KAFKA

De bustibus non est disputandum: Toplessness is now legal.

PAUL DAVY

Con sequitur: Parole officer.

IAN BROWN

Quip pro quo: Leave the jokes to the comedians.

RON CHARACH

Mea cuppa: Excuse me, but you're drinking my tea.

GEOFF WILLIAMS

Embarras de choux: Too much cabbage.   ALLISEN BELIER

Ag infinitum: The Prairies.   RENE JAMIESON

Pox Britannia: Mad cow disease.

MICHAEL & SANDI GREENE

Pro bozo publico: A real clown of a legal-aid lawyer.

JOHN LINGARD

Carve blanche: I'll have white meat, please.

MYRIAM PYETT

Joke de vivre: Life's funny that way.
Pot-au-few: Not many inhaled.   ALANNA LITTLE

Plus ça change, plus c'est la même close: Bankers' hours.

MICHAEL MCGLINCHEY

Pasta la vista: Spaghetti as far as the eye can see.

CARLOS NORONHA

Cur bono: What a nice doggie.　　　PAUL DUNSEATH

Whacun à son gout: Hit him on his sore foot.

BRADLEY CRAWFORD

Mom juste: Mother's had a few too many.

DOMINICK AMATO

Mott in Himmel: Applesauce to die for.　　STEPHEN SWARTZ

Tempus figit: These are restless times.　　BETSY NEWBECK

Sturm und Drano: Blocked-sink remedies.　　ERIC KOSKY

Porpus delicti: Evidence of illegal tuna fishing.

CATHERINE VELASQUEZ

Mens sana in corpore tano: One smart lifeguard.

MARY & HAROLD ATKINSON

Name That Disease

The broader the contest, the more people who enter. That, and the continuing national discussion about the state of publicly funded health care, prompted legions of readers to enter this contest: Take an existing medical condition, distort it while ensuring it remains recognizable and give the diagnosis. George Ramdial, who suggested the idea, offered the examples of fleabitis (an uncomfortable itch caught from household pets), romatism (a stressful condition caused by traffic paralysis in Rome) and thumbosis (a severe pain caused when the hammer misses the nail head; usually accompanied by a vulgar expression).

David Peetz, a visiting professor from Australia at Quebec's Laval University, offered an impressive catalogue of new ailments that had no chance of fitting into the column (I used one excerpt), but that fits nicely here.

I write to express my deep concern about the health of modern politicians. We have always known, of course, that when entering politics, most already suffer from influentia (pain caused by constantly speaking half-truths, though oddly the pain is mainly felt by others). Ministers in defence-related portfolios are particularly prone to chronic fatigues syndrome (a desire to dress up in army uniforms and perform strange acts with military equipment and cameras). But worst of all, I fear, is *AIDS* – Acquired Immunity from Deficiency Syndrome (a delusional state in which the sufferers come to believe that they can do not wrong, and have never done any wrong).

It is no surprise, then, that most end up with Anelection nervosa (a paralyzing fear of losing one's seat, the next time one stands). I hope that, through your column, you can draw attention to the plight of these people internationally, and work towards their being treated in the manner they so dearly need.

We do our best. Here, then, a partial list of ailments:

AsMa: Female problem; stress caused by discovering you are turning into your mother.   ANN TETLEY

Carpool tunnel syndrome: Fear of being in a dark, confined space with screaming children.
                                        CLAIRE MERANDA & ROD GOLDBERG

Newmoania: Tendency to find fault with anything modern.
                                                        PETER PERRYMAN

Pollio: Crippling need to know the opinions of others.
                                                        BRIAN D. JONES

Artrightis: A compulsion to straighten pictures on the walls of homes one visits.   ALANNA LITTLE

Peptalk ulcer: Intestinal pains brought on by attendance at Blue Jays strategy meetings.
                                        JOHN ILLINGWORTH & NORMA CRAWFORD

Hep-hepatitis: Disease of hyperactive cheerleaders.
                                                        FRANCES SLAYTON

Guestritis: Stomach disorder brought on by visits from the in-laws.

Pluralcy: Being beside oneself.   BARRIE COLLINS

Mad vow disease: Progressive cognitive impairment in the bride after a marriage ceremony.   CHERYL MINUK

mad vow disease

Boursitis: Fear of a stock-market crash.   GWEN WILKS

Birdsightis: Painful neck condition caused by compulsive searching for winged creatures.   BILL PLUMB

Tackycardia: Confusion in choice of greetings.   KEN DOWNING

Electile dysfunction: National ennui due to lack of good leadership candidates.   BOB HOUSELL

Brrrrsitis: Severe frostbite. LAREA MOODY

Keptomania: Fear (usually male) of throwing away any of
one's possessions. MARILYN PENNER

Hummeroids: Muscle aches from bouncing around in a
monster car on country roads. NANCY GEFFKEN

Hembolism: Shortness of breath, sweaty palms and loss of
rational articulation upon seeing teenage daughter's new
skirt. CAM FRENCH

Irritable vowel syndrome: Common compulsion among
country singers to fake an Ozarks accent. KEVIN SCULLY

Insolomia: Inability to sleep because you can't get that tune
out of your head. PETER GORHAM

Bicpolar disorder: The inability to write with a ballpoint
pen. C.H. VANE-HUNT

Mallaria: A compulsion to sing in shopping centres.
GARY E. MILLER

Spayback: When your cat accidentally neuters the vet.
JOHN HARRIS

INSECURELY YOURS

T he Challenge was to suggest unmistakable signs of insecurity or low self-esteem. Meg Sullivan, one of a handful of regulars from the United States, wrote, "Um, well, I did have a few ideas for this week's Challenge, but, well, they probably aren't very good – certainly not as good as everyone else's. You probably wouldn't want to see them anyway. I'm really sorry to have wasted your time. Thanks."

Shirley Grant introduced her entry (below) this way: "Here's my first entry to Challenges. It's not very good, but maybe if I keep trying, I'll improve."

Particularly in the early years, I was insecure about the very transference of the Challenge to the page. The Globe and Mail's editors are very good at catching mistakes. Trouble is, the Challenge is littered with intentional mistakes, on the order of Kay Dills's contribution to a list of books that didn't make it past the starting gate: Webster's Dictionary.

Some readers were similarly insecure in the early days about whether their entries had reached the Globe. The same entry would be sent by mail and by fax, just to be sure.

Occasionally, technology intruded. B.W. Jackson sent a follow-up letter after entering one contest. "The fourth item on my submission for Challenge 346 was not all there. Lest you form the opinion that I may be in a similar condition, let me explain that the shortcoming *resulted from my continuing ineptitude in the use of a word-processor rather than from an impression that the item as submitted formed a rhyming couplet. The item should have read: 'The Song of the Open Road's not an appropriate tune/ When heading north on a holiday weekend in June.' I have a habit of resting my hand on the space-bar while pausing for thought. This results in unexpected deletions. How they pass undetected is not so easily explained."*

Ken Purvis reported a technological epiphany of his own. "Wow! I've been using this computer for over a year, and that's the first time I've seen accents added, completely unbidden. I didn't know my font included accents. Maybe the computer really deserves to replace the quill pen after all. Now I have to find out how to tell it to place accents when I want it to."

I know how he feels. I have been using the Word program while assembling this book, and, rather than shut off the automatic prompts, have had to keep telling the computer that I want to spell humour with a u and that all these run-on sentences, misspellings and bizarre constructions are intentional.

And how can you tell whether you're insecure? Well . . .

You wear a name tag on your wedding dress.
You sign your full name when you write to your parents.

MARILYN PENNER

When you win at solitaire you assume you must have been
   cheating.
You think your passport photo is flattering.
When carving the Christmas turkey, you serve yourself the
   neck.   ALANNA LITTLE

You add an antacid to anything you are cooking.

LESLIE G. ANDREWS

You have a vanity licence plate, but it's blank.

CHARLES CROCKFORD

You agree to write that letter for the boss – the one that tells
you he's firing you. GORDON FINDLAY

You have a tattoo that says, "I plan to have all these tattoos
removed." LORRAINE FAIRLEY

You stop at a green light to let drivers on the red light go
first. GARY E. MILLER

When you call for an ambulance, you apologize to the 911
operator for disturbing her. SARAH FELDMAN

You take motivational videos on your honeymoon.
COLIN EYSSEN

You ask your dog to take you on its evening walk.
KEN PURVIS

You're working on your black belt in kowtow.
BARRIE COLLINS

The trial judge filed an appeal of her own judgment.
WENDY MULLIGAN

When you hear your name being paged, you assume there
must be another Vladimir Ho-Chi Amadeus Yamashita
staying at the same hotel.   BRIAN YAMASHITA

You use a breath mint after drinking water.
Before checking out of a hotel room, you fold the toilet
paper back into a point.   PAUL DAVY

You walk beside your horse so you won't be a burden.
You want to abbreviate your initials.   HELEN PERRY

You send Christmas cards and letters to yourself, hoping to
impress the mailman.   IAN GUTHRIE

You hire a limousine when it's your car-pool turn.
JOHN A. MILES

While watching the Grey Cup on TV, you complain that
when the teams were discussing strategy they were in
fact gossiping about you behind your back.
MALCOLM FLOWERDAY

You send out thank-you notes for junk mail.
WILLIAM M. VANCE

You write to your twin brother to remind him of your
birthday.   GEOFF WILLIAMS

With your party invitations you offer door prizes and
promise to pay taxi fares.   K.C. ANGUS

You apologize to a sidewalk cyclist for getting in his way.
ERIC ADAMS

You custom-print rejection slips and submit them with
your unsolicited manuscripts.   P.B. HAWKSHAW

You go to the police station to confess to driving over the
   speed limit.   ANDREW WEEKS

You arrive half an hour early for a meeting with someone
   who invariably arrives half an hour late.
                                          SHIRLEY GRANT

CULT DE SAC AND OTHER FOREIGN ADD-ONS

Many of the best challenges begin with a simple math problem: Add x to known quantity y and make the whole funnier than the parts. For instance, Gordon Findlay wrote, "The other day, when preparing a statement, I inadvertently put an s in front of the word 'invoice.' I looked at 'sinvoice' and thought, 'That describes the Visa receipt for a motel weekend with your secretary.'" He offered an example. Cadmiration: enjoying the exploits of absolute rotters.

Glen Acorn offered a more specific variation. Suppose you added a single letter to a familiar, non-English expression and redefined it. You might, as Mr. Acorn did, expand mea culpa to mega culpa: I'm really, really guilty. Or change pas de deux to spas de deux: two-seater hot tubs.

I dangled the bait before the Challengers, and they not only rose to it but darn near tore my arm off in their zeal. Abby Lippman, after a long list that included some treats (port favor: request for an after-dinner drink), added: "And finally, before completely wearing out your patience, some variations on a theme around Japanese food." These included slushi (wet rice roll) and subshi (rice roll served on Italian bread).

If anyone misses the Virgil reference in what follows, "facilis descensus averni" means the descent to Hell is easy. The reverse trip is murder, even with a gearshift.

Wendy Barker wrote, "This week's Challenge immediately brought to mind the quandary we face almost every day with two dogs and a vehicle with only room to take one." Her offering was carpet diem: *Which dog's turn is it to ride in the car today?*

This contest holds the record for number of columns mined from a single contest: the initial batch, and three sequels in quick succession. The use of sequels not only permitted the inclusion of terrific entries that couldn't fit the first time round, but allowed me to get away occasionally on holiday. In that order of importance, of course.

Among the other foreign expressions with a little bit extra:

Cult de sac: A sect with no future.
Ma foil: Straightman.
Carper diem: Perpetual whiner.   TIM & MAY ROWLAND

Joyeux nobel: The international prize for happiness.

MARGARET CLAYTON

Perp diem: New police arrest quota.

NORMA CRAWFORD & JOHN ILLINGWORTH

Meat culpa: Lapsed vegetarian.   CHERRY WATSON

Squid pro quo: Who ordered the calamari?

MARGARET MUNRO

squid pro quo

Snub judice: Scofflaw.
Chacun à son grout: Tile-setting for dummies.
Embarras de brichesses: Unzipped.   K.C. ANGUS

Add nauseam: Plus GST and PST.   AL WILKINSON

Ein prosite: A really professional Web page.
Cogito, ergo slum: I design low-cost housing.

BARRIE COLLINS

Orbiter dicta: Astronaut small talk.   JAMES FORSYTH

Halter ego: My friend thinks she looks great in a skimpy
    top.
Vex officio: Annoy the guy in charge.   VIVIAN BERARD

N'imported: Home-grown.   ISABEL HUNT

Scantabile: A Britney Spears performance.   KAY PERCIVAL

Phax vobiscum: You've got mail.
Pro bongo publico: Benefit concert.
Ahoi polloi: All sailors welcome.   MARK ECKENWILER

Bad infinitum: Dangerous offender. SHEILA HOLZER

Patter familias: I recognize your footsteps.
JEAN KALLMEYER

Tübermensch: Mr. Potato Head. TIM GOLDHAWK

Comme il faust: Devil-may-care. ANNE RONEY

Lad infinitum: Peter Pan. ROSALIND COOPER-KEY

Arse gratia artis: Meaningful nude scene. NATALIA MAYER

Financé: A rich prospective husband. MAURICE WHITBY

Facilis descensus taverni: It's an easy road down to the pub.
MALCOLM FLOWERDAY

Bona fride: Start of the Easter weekend. JULIET SMITH

Net cetera: Web trivia. ANNE SPENCER

Majordoomo: Nostradamus. KATHY POWER

Sex cathedra: Making out in church. DAVID READ

Bond mot: Secret agent's witticism. YVON MORENCY

Add hominem: Yes, we can squeeze one more person on this
elevator. DAVID TOPPER

Dulce et decorum est pro pastria mori: It is sweet and filling
to die for one's dessert. JEFF FORGRAVE

Pert capita: A cute hat.
Ad shoc: Tasteless publicity. ESTHER FINE

Phrosit: The schnapps is in the freezer.
À la cartel: Weekend gas pricing. NICK FURGIUELE

Compost mentis: Dirty mind. FRANCES PHILLIPS

Veni, vidi, Vinci: I came, I saw, I transformed the Italian
Renaissance.
In vino verbitas: Drunks talk too much. JOHN LAZARUS

Souse-chef: Cooking with alcohol.
LARRY & MADELEINE LEFEBVRE

Pierce de résistance: A nose-ring fitting gone horribly
wrong. DON RECCHI

Shabeas corpus: Poorly dressed body. FRED MOYES

Smuchas gracias: Thanks for the kisses.
Moan ami: Lover. BRUCE ZIFF

Faux past: Overimaginative CV.
Bonk appétit: Nymphomania. IAN CAMERON

O la law: Police pin-up calendar. HEATHER MACDONALD

Fibid: Plagiarist's footnote. CAMERON FRENCH

Honi soit qui male y pense: Honey, it's a guy thing.
Annoy domini: Eat the apple, Eve.
HELEN & PETER MARUCCI

Mens read: *Playboy*. GEORGE DUNBAR

B'sotto voce: Love song.
Chemin de fear: Formerly British Rail. CLAIRE WEEKS

Wunderbarn: The cows give chocolate milk.

LENORE DODICK

Deus hex machine: God has put a curse on my car.
Cab initio: The first taxi in the queue.
Chezi moi: Those are my Cheezies!
Père diem: Father's Day.

GLEN ACORN

Recognizing *a good premise when it saw one, the Challenge asked on another occasion for the addition of a letter to a famous person's name. This led to a mistake. One of the printed entries imagined Jaune Grey as the colourful wife of Henry VIII – which would have been funnier if Jane Grey had actually been one of Henry's wives. Here are a few of the legit entries:*

Lazyarus: Couldn't be bothered to get up from the dead.

ERIC MENDELSOHN

Divan the Terrible: A bad furniture-maker.

KATHY WILLIAMS

Mary, Queen of Scouts: A monarch whose motto was "Be prepared."

GEOFF WILLIAMS

Peter Plan: A man who won't grow up but will at least make a commitment.

SUE COOPERSTOCK

Schurbert: Composer famous for his sweets.

NATALIA MAYER

Victor Huggo: Touchy-feely French author. J.A. D'OLIVEIRA

NEOLOGISMS

Yes, *the English language is chockablock with words, but there is a crying need for new ones.* CBC *Radio aired an entire series, "Wanted Words," whose goal was to find the perfect single word to describe a hitherto unnamed concept or artifact. The Challenge has waded into the same waters, before and since, and developed a dictionary of incalculable utility. Bob Templeton set the ball rolling in 1992 by suggesting the invention of new words for our times, and by suggesting as his example "errato-ambulation": the tendency of people to walk directly into you, apparently because they have not seen you.*

At around the same time, Bob Levey's column in the Washington Post *painted a scene in which Joe and Michelle have shared a night of passionate love. The next morning, he wakes up and whispers, "I'll never forget last night, Gloria." What do you call the awkward moment that follows? The winning answer, from Holly McMullen: "Cadaschism."*

Unlike the other contests, which defined an object or notion and asked listeners to name it, the Challenge left both elements up to the readers. This made the project simultaneously easier (anything goes) and more difficult (anything goes, where do I start?). Simon Mortimer wrote a postscript to his entries: "The Challenge, which reminds me of the one in the Independent's *weekend magazine, is an amusing way to spend a Saturday morning when I should be studying for my examinations!"*

A few of the words and phrases that follow come from a 1999 Challenge that solicited names for interesting physical, psychological and social behaviour. Zachary Jacobson offered "Knee-jerk Challenge Delusion: the absolute certainty that if you do not personally enter a joke to every newspaper column or Internet joke list, the sun will not rise tomorrow!" Joseph E. Donnelly, who suggested the contest, supplied an example (included below) that drew this note from Ken Purvis: "I think you are allowing us to mix Latin and Greek roots! You'll probably get several 'Shocked and Appalled' letters from your more pedantic fans."

Here, then, the Random Dictionary:

Acronesia: Forgetting what an often-used acronym stands for.   STEPHEN HAYDEN

Afterquote: A quotation from the character or personage who said it second, third or later.   JAMES PALMER

Amber-despondency: The realization that you can't catch the green.
Bigrin's reflex: Spasm caused by receipt of phone call postponing a dental appointment.   K.C. ANGUS

Boomerangst: Midlife anxiety that is hard to get rid of.
                                                      ALANNA LITTLE

Coitius: The act of safe sex.   SIMON MORTIMER

Constipatution: The state of being unable to move one's country toward unity.   JOHN & LINDA KORT

Didya-view: The odd sensation, when someone is describing a movie, that you may or may not have seen it already.   FRANK MORGAN

Dysamicitia: The tendency to confuse friends with one
another. JOSEPH E. DONNELLY

Dysrexia: Being able to hear, but not understand, Rex
Murphy. KARL DILCHER

Fetashism: The inability to enjoy food unless it is sprinkled
with goat cheese. BRIAN EVANS

fetashism

Flicker-amnesia: Affliction of people who drive for miles at
a time with the turn signal on. DALE SCAIFE

Jix: To capriciously cast off a lover by fax. FRANK SCHOEN

Lemo: A limo with recurring mechanical problems.
ED KAMPS

Phonesia: The inability to remember who you just called.
LAUREN TELENCOE

Plasticitis: Tendency to exceed one's credit-card spending
  limits.   SUSAN OPLER

Rinkmanship: The art of negotiating professional hockey
  deals just before the playoffs.   JOHN & LINDA KORT

Sarandipity: The good fortune to find just enough plastic
  wrap on the roll to cover the leftover cucumber salsa.
                                            PHILIPPA HUNTER

Scriptoventilation: The tendency to blow on pencils after
  sharpening them.   PAUL DAVY

Stonewalker: A person who walks through a cemetery,
  reading the information from the headstones.
                                          DARREL E. KENNEDY

Tattleglow: Pride in ability to recall juicy details from TV
  shows.   DAVID DUNSMUIR

Versace second: The time that elapses between your buying
  a garment and its going out of style.
                                          CHARLES CROCKFORD

Walkman fallacy: The belief that you are speaking quietly to
  yourself, wearing earphones, when in fact you are shout-
  ing to hear yourself over the music in your ears.
                                          ZACHARY JACOBSON

Yoyo-nap: Head action of a sleeping subway rider.
                                              DALE SCAIFE

Is Everybody Happy?

A *curious feature of the Challenge, which I notice only in retrospect, is that variations on a similar idea tend to bunch up. In the middle of 1997, the Challenge was to suggest good-news spins to bad-news stories. A Challenge one year later was to suggest happy endings for well-known stories. A year after that, the Challenge was to put a positive spin on a bad situation. A couple of months after that, the Challenge was to celebrate the 1990s' genius for putting a positive spin on the definitions of business practices.*

This may speak to an air of determined optimism at the time, or an inattentive Challenge editor, or the psychological truth that new ideas feed on old ones. In practice, although all four ideas were essentially riffs on the good-news, bad-news joke, they were different enough that they brought in fresh answers.

Chris Knight and Monique Holmes proposed the initial Challenge after reading an article about Ontario's new (at the time) Highway 407. When the highway's tolling technology proved incapable of handling the number of drivers using the road, and no tolls could be collected, a spokesperson called the unmanageable volume "a good-news story just beyond our dreams."

The Challengentsia rose to the Challenge.

"The beauty of living here is that, if you miss garbage day, the city landfill is just over your back fence."

GEORGE E. JACKSON

"My stockbroker hardly ever bothers me since he put me into Bre-X."

JOHN MCKAY

"Hitting the windshield sure fixed my overbite."

DON TYRRELL

"This expected asteroid hit will give Mother Nature a chance to start over again."

KARL DILCHER

"On the other hand, Mrs. O'Leary, your cow was barbecued to perfection."

JEFF MCCARTNEY

A lanna Little was similarly struck by comments whose tone was positive but whose content was anything but. Her examples: "You are still No. 1 on our waiting list." "These salary cuts mean you'll pay less income tax next year." Among the submitted lines: "The greatest psychiatrist in the world is interested in your case" (R.G. Donner). "This is your captain speaking. The gentleman who has commandeered the plane has instructed us to divert from London and proceed to Kabul, and to credit everyone with 3,500 bonus Air Miles." (T.W. Morley).

Ron Charach was intrigued by what business could camouflage with a new, chipper vocabulary. His example: Calling up people you barely know and pestering them is called "networking." Other readers decoded similar terms. Exporting arms manufactured without the use of child labour is "business ethics" (Karl Dilcher). An inability to concentrate is "lateral thinking" (Barrie Collins). Cost-cutting is "reorganizing to serve our customers better" (Colin Eyssen). And, from Walter Shankman, "Using your touch-tone telephone, you will be presented with an ever-expanding menu of options that will lead you inevitably to complete confusion and frustration." This is called "customer service."

40

Ken Purvis suggested his challenge after reading a cartoon by Seymour Chwast that invented happy endings for such works as Gone With the Wind *(Scarlett saves Tara by turning it into a coffee bar) and* A Tale of Two Cities *(Sidney Carton uses the guillotine as an apple-peeler and wows the crowd). Among the happy-go-lucky revisions:*

The clever fox, in his attempts to reduce hydrogenated oil shortening and other forms of saturated fats found in his diet, declined to eat the Gingerbread Man.

HELEN ALEXANDER

Cain became an able lawyer and had his parents' expulsion overturned.

KARL DILCHER

It was revealed that, Mellors and Sir Clifford having been switched at birth, the gamekeeper is actually Sir Oliver Chatterley.

KEN PURVIS

King Arthur went for the square table, leaving no room for Sir Lancelot.

LESLEY HANDS WILSON

Lear: Thanks for your honesty, Cordelia. I really respect that.

RAMONA LUMPKIN & WILLIAM BLACKBURN

The wolf saw the errors of his ways, became a vegetarian, and helped the Three Little Pigs build their truck garden into an international tofu-marketing cartel.

In *Casablanca*, Paul Henreid turned out to be a Nazi double agent, Ingrid Bergman left him and she and Humphrey Bogart moved to Las Vegas where they opened a casino just in time to cash in on the postwar boom.

Hansel and Gretel filed a class-action suit against the witch for child abuse. She was rehabilitated, changed her name to Laura Secord and the rest, as they say, is history.

PETER MARUCCI

On his way to the old woman pawnbroker's, Roddy
Roskolnikov spotted a newspaper article declaring that
the Russian banks had decided to grant an amnesty on
all defaulting student loans.   RON CHARACH

The Old Man and the Sea: Instead of waiting for his catch to
be devoured by sharks, the old man pulled out a bottle of
soy sauce and a tube of wasabi and proceeded to carve
up the fish and make sashimi for his luncheon. EARL LIU

Godot got his own Web site.   JOHN O'BYRNE

So Dorian took his picture to a retoucher. . . .
                                               BARRIE COLLINS

Hamlet discovered that Ophelia had actually been enjoying
a herbal bath, and was now safe but damp.
                                    DICK & SUE WATERMAN

ophelia had been enjoying a herbal bath

Also *from the Watermans, a verse:*

> The boy stood on the burning deck
> Whence all about had fled.
> A rainstorm put the fires out.
> So he went back to bed.

And *S.F. Sommerfeld offered an alternative to "the fatal shootout in the Malamute saloon between Dangerous Dan McGrew and the Stranger from the Creeks." This one wouldn't fit into the column, so I'm delighted to use it here.*

> "'A Hound of Hell,'" McGrew protests,
> "But that is most untrue,
> For you confuse me with a louse
> Who's also named McGrew.
> His first name's Don, and I confess
> That he is my twin brother.
> Sometimes our parents couldn't tell
> The one son from the other.
> So please accept my deep regrets
> For all that Don has done,
> Nor blame the gentle Dan McGrew,
> The nobler, kinder one.
> So have a drink with Lou and me,
> You really made me nervous.
> I wasn't scared, but you'll agree
> You can't trust Robert Service."

HAIKU HAIKU OKAY

The Challenge cuts corners. I admit it. There are times when, for brevity and ease of explaining the rules, the contest does not always demand of readers what a stickler for detail might. In the case of double-dactyl poems, known colloquially as "higgledy piggledy" poems, because that's often their first line, one of the lines should according to the strict rules be a single word. I figure that if people want to create a humorous poem with the right metre and a single-word line, more power to them. I'm happy to get a combination of the first two.

With haiku, however, I wandered into the field in blissful ignorance. The Japanese verse follows a set pattern: five syllables in the first line, seven in the second, five in the third. Somebody, perhaps one of the other competitions in the world, had compiled a series of computer-error messages written as haiku, and a list of the better ones circulated on the Internet for many months, being traded back and forth between amused readers in the manner of found Internet material. Naturally, it had also been stripped of any sign of authorship. The Internet should fly a skull-and-crossbones flag and have a parrot on its shoulder.

If haiku could embrace computer errors, I figured, why not other seemingly incompatible forms? So I asked, in order, for haiku about U.S. President Bill Clinton's covert sexual experiences with intern

Monica Lewinsky; about household appliances; and about the Polar Lander, a spacecraft that NASA had apparently lost on Mars.

The results were quite wonderful, and will appear in a moment. However, a couple of readers more knowledgeable than I am immediately wrote to take issue with the word "haiku."

Yes, a haiku is a Japanese verse form, and yes, its metre is as advertised. However, wrote John A. Frow after the Clinton contest, "haiku is a treasure devised to demonstrate beauty and beautiful feelings. Haiku can include flowers, clouds, trees, insects, crabs, mountains, fog, reflections, sunbeams, snow, summer, heat and thousands of other natural things and phenomena. What all those fine poets who participated in your challenge were really crafting was a different type of poem called senryu. Senryu is usually about crimes against the state." He added, "Basho, a founding father of haiku, is turning over and over and over in his grave."

Mr. Frow was not alone. Fred Kerner, who as a publisher had commissioned Roy Copperud's A Dictionary of Usage and Style and could be expected to know his way around a point of style, similarly wrote that haiku, "while it does require the 5–7–5 syllable format, also calls for the subject matter to be nature and requires that there be a reference to a season. The form of verse (ku means verse in Japanese) in the same syllabic structure without the nature/season references is called senryu."

Ann Goldring, a founding member of Haiku Deer Park in Toronto, attached an essay she had written exploring the nuances of the haiku. "It is incorrect to equate the seventeen onji typical of the classical Japanese haiku with seventeen syllables in English. To capture the spirit of Japanese haiku, modern poets writing in English usually think in terms of one breath-length, giving rise to haiku of fewer than seventeen syllables. Not that we count. Nor do we count the number of lines; three is most common, but it is not unusual to find haiku of one, two or four lines." She added, "Far more important, a haiku must evoke a sense of awe, something your 'quivering toaster' fails to do."

That last reference was to the example provided by Hugh Quetton, who suggested the Challenge on haiku of praise to household appliances:

The toaster quivers,
Planning a personal best.
Toast on the ceiling.

*My only excuse is that the Challenge takes second place to no
one when bending the rules, or, where the rules are more fluid, creating rules where none should exist. As Steve Martin said, comedy
is not pretty.*

*First up, then, are Clinton senryu masquerading as haiku. Readers
should keep in mind, if only under protest, two of the seamier details
of his dalliance with Ms. Lewinsky: the stained dress that figured in
evidence at his impeachment, and the story that one of his cigars was
used in a licentious manner. Memo to younger readers: This is
history. You can look it up. Alanna Little sensed the dangers in a footnote to her entries:*

Entrants are challenged
To maintain the dignity
Of the Globe *Challenge.*

*Here, then, the verses Clinton might have sent to apologize for his
indiscretion:*

My impeachment woes
May pale in light of this fact:
The blue dress was mine.   JULIA WEISSER

I can't help it if
The Republicans have
No sense of humidor.   BARRIE COLLINS

My life is like golf
Because I've learned that in both
It's my lie that counts.   CHARLES CROCKFORD

I wish, I wish I'd
Never known that a thong was
Other than a shoe.   MARGARET TOTH

If I did a wrong,
I will drown myself, I swear,
In the typing pool.   CHARLES CROCKFORD

Gennifer, Paula,
Monica . . . Like my wife says,
"It takes a village."   BRIAN PASTOOR

Yet they believed Jack
When he said his sore back was
Due to overwork.   ZENON YARYMOWICH

The dress you will see
Hang in the Smithsonian:
The Shroud of Clinton.   J.T. CURRIE

nd now, the odes to household appliances:

My toaster is not
The greatest thing since sliced bread
Which it burns daily.   BARRIE COLLINS

Do you eat my socks?
Is that how they disappear?
Dryer, speak to me!

        NORMA CRAWFORD & JOHN ILLINGWORTH

Oh hear my juicer.
"Pandemonium!" it cries.
Undetected pit.   JONI DUFOUR

vcr flashes
12 12 12 incessantly.
Where's the teenager? WENDY MARTINDALE

Brave the bathroom scale.
Nothing ventured, nothing gained.
Nothing lost, either. TRACY TAYLOR

Brave the bathroom scale...

Vacuum cleaner hums,
Busy, busy. In closet
Old broom smiles and waits. B.W. JACKSON

Stove's blackened again.
Microwave has exploded.
Perhaps I can't cook. JULIE VIDA

Ms. Vida, I should note, was a student at Forest Heights Collegiate Institute in Kitchener, Ontario. Hers was among several I received *from a class taught by Mandica Horne, who sent them in with a note: "After the literacy test was cancelled, my Grade 10 English classes welcomed the weekly Challenge. I hope you enjoy these!" A few teachers have sent similar batches over the years, and there is usually gold to be mined from them.*

And finally, the Mars haiku (I am cheating here and thinking of Mars as nature). The U.S. National Aeronautics and Space Administration hadn't heard from the Polar Lander since it reached Mars, so the challenge was to suggest a message that NASA might have received in the previous week – from Mars, from the craft, from whomever or whatever – on this subject.

Good news: found water.
Bad news: quicksand. Am sinking.
Winch-truck wants spot cash.   JAMES F. DOIG

No water on Mars
But the alternative is
Red, white, sweet or dry.   ANYA BOSNICH

Thanks for the present.
We opened it on Sunday.
It was delicious.   ROSS DOUGLAS

Nothing to report.
Nothing really to report.
Not a thing, really.   F.W. MORGAN

Everything went well
Until we came to the hard
Red rock at the end.   PETER GREEN

I have not arrived
Because I have never left.
You must search harder.   J.A. BERGBUSCH

What a lovely gift!
Merry Christmas to you too.
We didn't have one.

MURIEL DUMARESQ

Just heard from Venus.
They have your Polar Lander.
Improve your aim, eh?

HOLLY ANDREWS

When it reached the sand
My children heard the motors.
They killed and ate it.

MICHAEL DAVIES

What did you expect?
I was manufactured by
The lowest bidders.

BARRIE COLLINS

Mars is very cold.
I went to Saturn instead.
Don't wait up for me.

LORI RUTHERFORD

And a closing thought from reader Ash Shihora: "I am of the opinion that NASA does not always screw up. In fact, it may be that their robot was so perfect that it began to think for itself. I guess that I am just a romantic scientist with a poet's heart."

NOW WHERE DID I LEAVE MY SURGICAL SPONGE?

The public health-care system in Canada is such a source of wonder that in the opening years of the twenty-first century, at least four separate commissions – Fike, Romanow, Mazankowski, Kirby, forgive me if I've forgotten anyone – were sent out to find out how it was failing Canadians and how it might be fixed. There were verbal duels between people who said the system was better than anyone else's and people who wondered why their uncle had to wait three years for a hip replacement.

The Challenge knew grist for its mill when it saw it. In 1998, readers were asked to compose a note of explanation or excuse from a member of the health system to a disgruntled user. A few of those who responded were doctors, nurses and hospital administrators.

Catherine Barber wrote to add her "two cents' worth. As an RN in a very busy department, I'm privy to some rather dark humour at coffee breaks." She offered two examples. "1. In an effort to keep this hospital operational in the face of the nursing shortage, we have hired nurses back from retirement. Please respect their efforts as they manoeuvre with their canes and walkers. 2. The nurses in this department are committed to quality care. In an effort to achieve this, some nurses may be working twenty-four-hour shifts. Please consider their fatigue." She added: "These two themes are based on fact. Hopefully there is some humour seeping through."

51

Other notes of explanation or excuse:

"Yes, you should have a sore throat after that hernia operation. The hernia procedure went so well the students demanded an encore, so I removed your tonsils."

BRUCE MCFARLANE

"Please note that the doctor will be unable to make house calls, since he has left his car keys in a patient."

MUHAMMAD VELJI

"I can explain the parking tab. Surely you remember your stretcher being in the corridor for two and a half days?"

FRANK MORGAN

"Yes, the Emerg offers twenty-four-hour service, but not consecutively, and certainly not in a day."

MURI B. ABDURRAHMAN

"The Health Minister has redefined semi-private to mean two patients per bed."

BARRIE COLLINS

"Dear Ms. Jones: Following your unfortunate misunderstanding at the hospital, the janitor has been instructed not to wear a white coat."

BERT GASKELL

"Dear Mr. Caesar: We apologize for the foul-up. I am reasonably certain that had your name been anything other than Ian, we would have noticed that your patient name information had been erroneously entered on the 'surgical procedure' line."

DAN RAFFERTY

I *n 2001 we went back at the subject with a twist. The challenge was to show the health-care system was really cutting costs. Alanna Little attached a footnote to her submissions: "at the risk of providing even more ideas to some notable health-care innovators."*

After the column ran, a few readers got in touch to say that the more extreme lines weren't far from the truth. Said one, in a phone message: "About two years ago I was assaulted and received a very large gash in my head which required fourteen staples put into my skull without the benefit of anaesthetic. So I'm afraid that reader [an entry about anaesthesia] showed more practical experience than imagination or humour. We're already there for that one. Having the staples taken out was fun, too, as you might imagine. Much more interesting than having stitches taken out."

A second reader wrote: "Several years ago, I was being operated on for a hernia. The surgeon has a wicked sense of humour. The last thing I heard before I went under was his voice saying, 'Now let me see, which side was it on?'"

A third reader left this phone message: "We took our elderly mother-in-law, eighty-nine I believe she was, to the hospital about a year or so ago. Couldn't balance, couldn't sit, couldn't stand, figured it was middle ear or a stroke. They said, uh, nothing more we can do, take her home. We said, 'She can't even stand or walk, how are we going to get her up the stairs?' 'She can crawl, can't she?' I thought that was rather neat."

Here, then, are other, possibly fictitious signs of cost-cutting in the Canadian health-care system:

"You thought the optometrist recommended laser surgery?
I'm sure he meant to say razor."
"The price of anaesthesia has gone sky-high. Roy the Rodeo
Clown will distract you during your appendectomy."
"We can't actually send an ambulance, Mrs. Jones, but our
Web-site address is www.heartattack.com.

R. ALAN PERRY & J. BAILEY

"Your surgeon bears an uncanny resemblance to our auto
mechanic." SANDRA LLOYD

"If you want that monitor to keep working, you'll have to
pedal a bit harder, sir." ELLEN JOST

"All X-rays will be performed by the resident psychic."
COLIN EYSSEN

"You'll have to stay off that leg for at least a month, so there'll be plenty of time to whittle these two pieces of wood into crutches."
BRENDA WEIDE

"Hey, blood's blood, isn't it? Don't be so picky."
WARREN C. JACKSON

"For a $50 hospital donation, we could make this sponge bath both extra enjoyable and tax-deductible."
JERRY KITICH

"Actually, these aren't the X-rays of your broken leg, but we're going to use them to save on film."
FRANK N. SMITH

"There are great synergies with having the new funeral home next door."
PATRICK CAPPER

"Your new pacemaker is self-winding, so remember to keep moving."
BARRIE COLLINS

"We've had to reschedule your hip replacement. The operating theatre has been rented by the drama club."
R.M. BAXTER

"Bite down hard on this leather strap when I tell you."
MICHAEL SPIERS

"To cover the cost of the trip, ambulances will deliver pizzas when going to patients."
CHARLES CROCKFORD

"Our thoracic surgeons have found yet another use for duct tape."
KARL DILCHER

"I'm sorry, but everyone can't have a lower bunk."
"I know your cast seems heavy, but concrete is better for
   you than plaster."   AL WILKINSON

IT WAS A DARK AND STORMY CHALLENGE

The Challenge column has a set amount of space. If an advertisement falls through on a Wednesday, the editor may wander by and, struggling to keep panic from his voice, ask whether I might supply twice as many entries as usual. But in general I have to assume that if I asked readers to compose, say, a sonnet, there would be room for only a handful.

That wouldn't seem right, somehow. I'd be kept awake nights by a clutch of perfectly good sonnets banging on the door and demanding their due. So the longest poetic assignment I have set involved the double-dactyl verse, also known as "higgledy piggledy," examples of which appear in another chapter.

On those rare occasions when I relaxed the restrictions on prose length, the results were mixed. The column was in its infancy when I asked readers to write a modern Aesop's fable, and I'm convinced the assignment scared off many readers who might otherwise have become regulars. At any rate, there were only ten entries, of which three or four were good enough to print. There was room for two.

The winner was K.C. Angus of Kemptville, Ontario, who became one of the staunchest regulars. In fact, years later, for his eightieth birthday, his family compiled and bound for him a beautifully printed book of all his Challenge entries. His son and daughter-in-law, Ian and Lis Angus, invited me to write a foreword – a *singular honour – and I responded in the spirit of the Challenge with a poem:*

> *When God handed out wits of concrete,*
> *K.C. swallowed an exempt pill.*
> *And he must be awfully neat,*
> *Else he'd live in Unkemptville.*

The greatest avalanche of lengthy entries followed the request in 2000 for entertainingly awful opening sentences to a novel, which had to include the words "peach," "umbrella" and "perfect." The inspiration was the annual international Bulwer-Lytton writing contest, which celebrates (if that's the word) the talent of author Edward Bulwer-Lytton (1803–1873), who kicked off one of his stories with the memorable sentence "It was a dark and stormy night." (Considering his devotion to long, convoluted sentences, it's amusing that his best-known work, The Last Days of Pompeii, *was condensed to a comic book in the twentieth-century series* Classics Illustrated.*)*

Most of the submissions chose to parody those writers who don't know when, or even whether, to finish a sentence. Consider the winner, from Barbara Halladay:

> He looked across the table at his date and thought immediately that she had a face similar to a peach, only not in a good way like the characters in romance novels, meaning a perfect complexion that supposedly cannot be bought although it could if one spent enough on cosmetics, the expensive ones in particular, but more like a peach on a discount supermarket shelf in early autumn with soft brown bruises and lots of fuzz that you can't get out from between your teeth unless you pick it out with the pointy end of those little umbrella decorations that festoon fancy girly drinks.

A *few entries unashamedly filled a page. In fact, John A. Miles was such a glutton for punishment that he – well, let him tell it.*

After e-mailing my entry on July 16th, I started jotting down notes. Then I started tapping it into the computer. Following this is what I printed out this morning, the first chapter of my awful but hopefully entertaining "novel," with your three words also in its last sentence. Sorry for the layout, but it's my very first computer, a hybrid given to be as a birthday gift this January, and it didn't come with a manual.

Small wonder Terry Lovekin began his e-mail entry with this note: "With sympathy (no one should have to read as much bad prose as you will receive over this Challenge)."

Barrie Collins, who has a habit of attaching punning headings to his entries, outdid himself here: "How Dark and Stormy Was My Valley and Other Notes from the Bul-Lytton Board." Nick Furgiuele, whose entry played off T.S. Eliot's "J. Alfred Prufrock," added, "My apologies to Mr. Eliot and to you." Alanna Little, who regularly appends postscripts to her entries, wrote, "If you don't make the cut, is your entry too good to be bad enough, too bad to be good enough, or just really, really mediocre?"

Hard question to answer, but I'll let a few of the best/worst entries speak for themselves.

In hindsight, it should have been obvious that the space-based missile system was the perfect defensive umbrella against everything but a peach.   CHRIS MUELLER

Cursing Fifi LaFlamme for deliberately flinging her peach daiquiri onto the dangerously polished marble steps, Bond took a tumble but still managed to hold onto his government-issue umbrella-*cum*-grenade-launcher which, with perfect aim, he fired to simultaneously reduce the receding Jaguar's resale value, barbecue the notorious Vic Blowfly and create another "situation" for the Home Secretary.   RUTH STERN WARZECHA

The peach hit his umbrella with the soft plop a trout makes rising for a fly on a misty loch in Scotland, where golf is a passion that burns deep, like the love he'd had for Eloise before that swine Henderson had unexpectedly arrived in Catalonia to ruin their perfect summer.

GORDON FINDLAY

The handsome Dr. Hugh Devine strode purposefully into Emergency and, stopping only to admire his perfect profile and furl his damp umbrella, seized a scalpel and expertly lanced a painful boil shaped like a peach which had appeared on the rear of seven-year-old Jimmy Davies.

LIZ GIBBON

She opened her umbrella to shade her pale, peach-like complexion, and thinking what a perfect day it would be if only she'd remembered her shoes, began her barefoot trek across Death Valley. NANCY MOUGET

MINUS A LETTER

So much of language hangs on the addition or subtraction of a letter. A pleasant conversation may be chatty, an unpleasant one catty. It's better to lose yourself in a book than a brook. You'll meet with more harm from an awful act than a lawful one.

In that spirit, Challenge 424 asked readers to "remove a letter from any foreign-language expression" and define the result. The wording was infelicitous, as Glen Acorn reminded me from Edmonton. "Challenge 259 (changing a letter) and Challenge 411 (adding a letter) were discreet in referring to a 'non-English' expression, whereas Challenge 424 refers to a 'foreign-language' expression, indicating that entries based on a French expression are in a language foreign to Canada." Good catch on Mr. Acorn's part.

He also wrote, "In some cases, readers may be baffled as to which letter has been deleted from the entry." While I prefer to err on the side of too little explanation, I will observe that the original version of one of the following mangled phrases – "de minimis non curat lex" – means that the law does not concern itself with small things. I first heard the expression as the punchline of an off-colour joke, in the same vein as another joke that ends with the evidence not standing up in court. I won't trouble you with the details.

Ça ne fit rien: Who could get into these?
Tot d'abord: First child. PATRICK GAGE

Pas de dux: Dance of the waterfowl. ANNALISE ACORN

pas de dux

De minimis non curat ex: Your wife wants the oak desk but
   doesn't give a damn about the jar of paper clips on it.
Chacun à son gut: Please don't tell me about your intestinal
   difficulties. ERIC MENDELSOHN

Ax vobiscum: You're all sacked. TONY ROBSON

Mea ulpa: Now I'm done for! RON CHARACH

Savoir fare: Having the right change ready.
CHERRY WATSON

Tot ensemble: Our Gang.
Dane macabre: Hamlet. VIVIAN BERARD

Buenos dis: A cheap shot, but a good one.

DAVID DUNSMUIR

Götterdämmerug: Blast, I've tripped on the carpet again.

BILL KUMMER

In loo parentis: Father cannot come to the phone at the moment.

COLIN EYSSEN

Pot mortem: Guess these plants needed more light.

BARRIE MOORE

Con bio: Inflamed résumé.

NORMA CRAWFORD & JOHN ILLINGWORTH

Cui boo?: Who disagrees?

CHRISTIAN STUHR

Asse-partout: A total jerk.
Ficionado: A fan of nuclear power.

NATALIA MAYER

Et tu, Brut: We're both wearing the same cologne.

EDWIN BOLWELL

Laissez aire: To pass wind.

ALLISON MILLER

Memento moi: I'll pay for the building if you name it after me.

CHARLES CROCKFORD

Que sera era: The age of apathy.

TRACIE BARNETT

Bric-à-bra: Antique foundation garment.

GORDON BLACK

Pêt à porter: Lapdog.

JOHN BART

Ice versa: Turn a cold shoulder to.

DAVID ANTSCHERL

N'est-ce pa: No, you're not the baby's father.

PETER CRANSTON

Eductio ad absurdum: Everyone gets a Ph.D.   JOHN MILLEN

A Head of Our Times

Headlines are the perfect Challenge form. They are brief, and may be attached to any subject, be it the working world, the Bible or the trials of Winnie-the-Pooh.

With Pooh, the spark was a news item in February 1998. British MP Gwyneth Dunwoody was fighting in the press for the return to Britain from New York of the stuffed toys that inspired A.A. Milne to write Winnie-the-Pooh. Readers were asked for better tabloid headlines than the one that ran in the New York Post: POOH ON YOU! Among the responses:

Odds of Pooh's Return Are a Milne-to-One.

GARY E. MILLER

Free the "Now We Are" Six!   BARRIE COLLINS

Brits Deplore "Bear of Very Little Brain" Drain.

CHERRY WATSON

Doug Brown had the inspired idea of asking readers for a biblical headline:

Shortage of Galilean Fishermen Blamed on Itinerant
Preacher. L. CHICHOCO

Noah Accused of Nepotism.
Three Wise Men to Pay Customs Duty on Imports.
CHERRY WATSON

Pharaoh Sets up Insect Task Force After Worst Locust
Plague This Century.
Pests Found in Apple Trees Again; Garden Closed Until
Further Notice. SIMON ELLIOTT PARKER

Judas Fined After Not Declaring Extra Income.
PAUL SHELLEY

"Communications Problem" Halts Construction on
Skyscraper. JANE WANGERSKY

Solomon Renders Split Decision in Custody Battle.
NICK VANDERVOORT

Animal-Rights Activists Condemn Proposal for Floating
Zoo. EDWARD BAXTER

Work Stoppage on Megaproject After Six Days Sets
Precedent. JACK ORBAUM

Carpenter Won't Fix Tables Damaged by Errant Son.
JIM PARR

B ert Gaskell *suggested asking for outlandish tabloid headlines in
the "startling new evidence" genre:*

DNA Tests Show Dionne Quints Not Related.
PATRICIA TRIPP

Hubble Pictures Prove Toronto Is Centre of Universe.

L.J. KOH

Ultrasound Technician Finds Box for Inner Voice.

PAM OSER

New Excavation at Oak Island Unearths Long-Buried
Canadian Identity. ROBERTA BAIRD

Blueprints Reveal CN Tower Is One of Many Supporting
Columns for Unbuilt Structure.

ROBERT & JANET NUNN

Radon Gas in Buckingham Palace Shown to Cause Royal
Marital Problems. COLIN EYSSEN

Twisters Can Read Your Mind.
Biologists Discover Couch-Potato Gene.

BRAM EENDENBURG

Land Survey Shows Pisa Leaning, Tower Vertical.

BARRIE COLLINS

Medical Journal Reveals Asbestos to Be Excellent Source of
Fibre for Healthy Eating. ROGER GUSTAFSON

Pavarotti X-Rays Shed Light on Disappearance of Carreras
and Domingo. RON CHARACH

NASA Confirms Men Are from Mars, Women Are from
Venus, Dogs from Pluto. ALANNA LITTLE

What's left? How about an occupational headline, one that
reflects the subject's job?

Greek Butcher Lambasted. SUSAN WEISS

Author Declares Chapter 11.
Priest Cross-Examined.   REBECCA ANHANG

Captain of Sinking Ship Denied Bail.   SANDRA FRAYNE

Local Optician Framed.   LENORE DODICK

Judge Condemns Chiropractor As Manipulative.
India Rubber Man Jailed for Long Stretch.   GLEN ACORN

Missing Real Estate Salesman Located, Located, Located.
Pawnbroker Gets Ticket, Redeems Himself.
                              BARRIE COLLINS

Baker Fired for Loafing.   B.W. JACKSON

Dentist's Defence Full of Holes.   MARILYN PENNER

Must Vintner Be Deported?   K.C. ANGUS

Robert Sproul *asked for headlines that sound far worse than the mundane stories that follow. His example was as extreme as they come: Millions Are Dead, on a story looking into Canada's cemeteries. But other readers gave him a run for his alarmist money, including William Gulycz, who wrote, "The following headlines simply must be true! Exclamation marks absolutely mandatory!!"*

Virtuoso Pianist Loses Hand! (He only held a pair of twos.)
                              KEN PURVIS

Countless Thousands Flee City Centre! (Evening rush hour.)
Thousands of Hectares of Shoreline Vanish Overnight!
(Tide rolls in.)   WILLIAM M. GULYCZ

Shark Handlers Cut in Half! (Sea World downsizes.)
                              PAUL DAVY

67

B.C. Codger Bemused! (Challenge contestant Barrie Collins admitted to our reporter that he didn't have his A-muse today but will submit entries anyway.) BARRIE COLLINS

A *complication in reprinting some of these Challenges is that the political references in the news may have been lost in the mists of time. That certainly applies to a Challenge set in 1999 that asked for headlines that might appear in a Canadian newspaper in 2000. It would take a couple of sentences to explain Chrétien Misses Yeltsin Funeral: Cites Golf-Cart Breakdown, though Lewis Abbott's winning entry was an incisive comment on the Canadian prime minister's weak excuse for missing an earlier state funeral. Similarly, Colin Eyssen's imaginative leap that Quebec might secede, then rethink its departure – Bouchard Insulted If Unable to Rejoin Canada – loses something now that Lucien Bouchard is no longer Quebec's premier.*

It's hard to remember that people in 1999 were petrified that computers unable to recognize the digits 2-0-0-0 would plunge the world into chaos, but that concern was behind Helen and Peter Marucci's entry: Compooters Stilllll Shewing Affects of Y2K Bugg.

Here's a taste of the more timeless candidates:

Last Tree in Canada Felled: Defunct Logging Industry
  Blames Ottawa. K.C. ANGUS

Ban on Cannibalism Overturned by Supreme Court: Cites
  Freedom of Religious Observance.

  DICK & SUE WATERMAN

Tim Horton's Sued by Overweight People, Claim
  Doughnuts Too Tasty. BRIAN EVANS

Newfoundland Frustrated Over Having to Give Transfer
  Payments to the Nine 'Have-Not' Provinces.

  ANDREW WEEKS

Late in 2001, the Challenge was to imagine what newspaper headlines might be like if this were a kinder, gentler world. This was barely two months after the terrorist attacks on the World Trade Center in New York, and there was much wishful revisiting of those events of September 11, including various scenarios in which Osama bin Laden did not exist. None made it into the column, since any wry humour that might have come with historical distance from the event was not yet in evidence. Among the entries that did see print:

Motorist Receives High-Five for Parallel Parking in Latest
  "Road Contentment" incident.
Woman Gets "Pretty Nice Haircut" in Drive-by Styling.

CHRIS KNIGHT

Rash of House Break-ins, Homeowners Delighted to Find
  New Televisions and VCRs.
Big Three Automaker Recalls Vehicles: CEO Says Nothing
  Defective, Just Found One or Two Ways to Make Them
  Run Better.

JERRY KITICH

Calgary and Edmonton Bury the Hatchet, Amalgamate into New City Called Calmonton.   CHARLES CROCKFORD

Megacorps Executives Admit Bad Planning, Lay Themselves Off.   BARRIE COLLINS

Epidemiologists Discover Something That Is Good for You.   COLIN EYSSEN

Corporate Sponsors of Eponymous Sport and Entertainment Complexes to Change the Names to Those of Dedicated Community Volunteers.   LINDA LUMSDEN

Charitable Institutions Say "Whoa," Suggest You Take a Vacation Rather Than Send a Donation, As They Have Sufficient Funds for the Next Few Years.   SANDRA WOODS

Banks Cancel Student Loan Repayments: "Just Seeing Them Graduate Is Enough."   MIKE ROWE

Unknown Man in Car Takes Child, Drives Her Home: "I Just Couldn't Let Her Endure That Rain. It's Too Wet to Be Outside."   SEAN BEGGS

Eminem Issues Lullaby Album.   BOB KINGSBURY

HIGGLEDY PIGGLEDY

To write a double-dactyl poem, known as "higgledy piggledy" after its opening line, requires a good sense of rhythm. There is only one rhyme, so that part isn't hard. I don't require, as some do, that one of the lines be a single word. But the rhythm – ah, you can't fake that. The metre must be "DA da da DA da da" for each of the eight lines except the fourth and eighth, whose metre is "DA da da DA." If the result makes sense and, better, makes the reader laugh, all is well.

I had not realized, until Irma Coucill sent me a clipping from the Ottawa Journal in 1993 of a review of the book Jiggery-Pokery by Anthony Hecht and John Hollander, that the two men had created the form. Their form was strict. Beyond the requirement that one of the lines ("ideally in the antepenultimate line") be a single word and that the opening line be sheer nonsense ("higgledy piggledy," "jiggery pokery"), they insisted that the second line be a double-dactylic name (such as Juliet Capulet), which would rule out many of the contributions I received. As well, they stipulated that once a single double-dactylic word had been used to fill a line, "it may never be used again." I chose to be more lenient, but would occasionally receive letters from readers saying the rules should be tightened to be true to the original design.

A 1995 double-dactyl Challenge brought this response from Paul Davy: "It was nice to have my double-dactyl published on the front *page of the Focus section on June 10. You made my day, but no doubt my wife found me insufferably vain."*

Two of the contributions here are from Jim Parr. He was an extraordinary man. When he died too young in April 2000, his obituary mentioned that he had been the host of CBC *Radio's* The Mad Metallurgist, *a university professor, director-general of the Ontario Science Centre, deputy minister of colleges and universities for the Ontario government, chairman of the public television network* TVOntario *and, yes, a regular Challenge entrant. He was particularly good at the verse Challenges, and wrote operatic libretti for the Arts and Letters Club in Toronto.*

After news of his death appeared, Alanna Little wrote, "Although I knew Jim Parr only through the Challenge and other occasional pieces in the Globe, *I admired him greatly. I have raised more than one glass in his memory and I'm sure you have too." And she quoted one of his Challenge poems: "Mozart or Haydn?/ It's difficult decaydn." Kurt Loeb, another regular, wrote to say that he and Jim had had a "friendly little challenge" each week to see which of them, if either, would manage to scale the Challenge walls.*

Quite a sterling bunch, this Challengentsia.

On with the double dactyls:

Higgledy piggledy
Julius Caesar went
Off to the Senate, though
Warned by a seer.
Brutus, defending his
Threatened Republic, in
Loco citato, stopped
Julie's career.   GLENDA BOCKNEK

Higgledy piggledy
Numa Pompilius,
Once King of Rome, had a
Peacekeeping touch.
Forty years passed without

Ever a battle. (And
That's perhaps why we don't
Hear of him much.)   JIM PARR

Higgledy piggledy
Alice in Wonderland
Said to her mother while
Taking a bath:
"Carroll has asked if he
Might take my photograph."
Ma said, "I'll tell him to
Stick to his math."   JIM PARR

Higgledy piggledy
Gabriel Fahrenheit.
Cold to the bone was he,
Needed new scale.
Raised it by thirty-two
Thermodynamically,
Snug as a bug at last,
Glowing, not pale.   KURT LOEB

Higgledy piggledy
Ludwig van Beethoven
Used to give concerts but
No one would come.
Got a new gimmick and
Standing-room only by
Starting a symphony
DA DA DA DUM.   JEAN HAMILTON

Higgledy piggledy
John A. Macdonald was
Proud that his railway gave
B.C. a link.
Asked if he planned to ride

73

Out to the coast, said he:
"Sure, if you promise to
Furnish the drink."

KEN PURVIS

Higgledy piggledy
Westward Magellan went,
Circled the world, oddly
Losing a day.
Deed without precedent!
All that the sailors said:
"What will that day we lost
Mean to our pay?"

K.C. ANGUS

Higgledy piggledy
Thirsty Count Dracula
Took his transfusions from
Folks he'd select.
Red Cross authorities
Frowned at his willfulness,
Putting the bite on the
Donors direct.

K.C. ANGUS

Count Dracula Blood Bank

Higgledy piggledy
Vlad the Impaler was
Irking the neighbours with
Mayhem and gore.
Said we acknowledge his
Right to his lifestyle but
Property values have
Gone through the floor.

JEAN HAMILTON

Higgledy piggledy
Biruté Galdikas
Swung from the chandeliers,
Climbed up the drapes.
Folks in Toronto said,
"This we won't tolerate."
Now she's in Borneo
Living with apes.

R.M. BAXTER

"Higgledy! Piggledy!
Bother and Fiddlesticks!"
Tricky Dick Nixon said,
"I'm not a crook!"
(If we'd included the
Rest of his expletives
This simple statement would
Fill a large book.)

BARRIE COLLINS

Higgledy piggledy
L.M. Montgomery's
Anne of Green Gables is
Known the world o'er.
Prince Edward Islanders
Think that its heroine,
Far from delightful, is
Really a bore.

BARRIE COLLINS

Sip-it-y, gulp-i-ty,
John A. Macdonald, Sir,
First of prime ministers,
Pickled his brain.
Nevertheless, working
Dipsomaniacally,
John A. Macdonald, Sir,
Gave us the Train.   ZACHARY JACOBSON

RODEO AND JULIETTE

Perhaps, in a weak moment, someone thought of staging The Vagina Monologues in Saskatchewan and renamed them The Regina Monologues. Perhaps a bored parishioner, halfway through a chorus of "Onward Christian Soldiers," wondered whether a subtle twisting of the title might not make it the perfect political rallying cry: "Onward Chrétien Soldiers." The Great Gatsby? That might work for the Americans, but think of the resonance in Canada if the book were rechristened The Great Gretzky.

The Challenge came from Leslie S. McKillop: Adapt the title of any non-Canadian book, song, play, movie, poem or painting to make it more typically Canadian. E.g. The Lyon King.

I was particularly touched by this note from Maynard Bates, who had tested out his equipment for the first time in New Victoria, Nova Scotia, and followed up with a typed letter. "I e-mailed this entry yesterday, but as I had never used e-mail before, I am sending this as insurance. If you received my e-mail entry, congratulations on being my first electronic contact."

It was worth it. He offered The Greatest Tory Ever Sold: John A. Macdonald and the Pacific Scandal. And Fahrenheit −45.1. And, in remembrance of Conrad Black, who had just cut his ties with Canada in order to accept a life peerage, Black Booty: Hollinger Inc. and the Publishing Industry.

A. Trevor Hodge confided that, "once started, I couldn't stop them coming." He volunteered The Moosetrap, Ein Klein Nachtmusik *and even* The Shopping News. *He explained away the incongruity of Canadianizing a book set in Newfoundland by pointing out that* The Shipping News *was, "after all, a U.S. film." What struck me more was the assumption that Canadians are keener shoppers than the Americans. I didn't use it for that reason; let the people in the malls fight that one out, I figured, not the folks writing letters to the* Globe.

Tonya Lowe wrote: "How my Australian friend (visiting Canada) and I enjoyed this Challenge!!" Perhaps the friend, Kate Ellis, was responsible for the variation on the Maurice Sendak children's book Where the Wild Things Are – Where the Mild-Mannered Things Are – *or Pierre Boulle's* Planet of the Ehs. *As others see us, etc.*

As usual with Challenges that can be answered with the twist of a letter, a great many people submitted precisely the same entries. Lord of the Rings *was a natural:* Lord of the Rinks. *Ken Purvis, offering* The Great Gretzky, *remarked in parentheses, "I expect you will get dozens of this one." He was right. A few readers proposed* My Fur Lady, *which had been taken decades earlier by a Canadian revue. Karl Dilcher recalled that the Royal Canadian Air Farce had performed a radio sketch on a supposed Newfoundland movie called* The Codfather.

Stockwell Day, who was running again to be leader of the Canadian Alliance after a fractious year in and out of the job (he lost), lent his name to any number of titles with Day in them. Best of them was Stock Day's Journey into Night.

And, as usual, where there were duplicates I flipped a coin. It keeps me honest, and keeps my thumb and forefinger limber.

Too bad the challenge didn't invite the Canadianizing of names of rock groups. Krista Peterson would have scored with Zed Zed Top. *And I felt a momentary pang on reading this postscript from Graeme Foster, whose entry was fine (*Two Gentlemen of Kelowna*) but who lost the coin toss. "I keep sending entries in to you which are never printed," he wrote. "Are you not receiving them? Are they really that bad? Are you the guy I gave the wedgie to in high school?" In order, the answers are yes, no and no.*

Here are a few other highlights (I have included a couple of entries to an earlier Canadianization challenge):

Rodeo and Juliette	ELSPETH FLOOD
Annie Get Your Gumboots	CHRISTINE L. COOPER
"Sir John A. Macdonald Had a Farm"	KURT LOEB

John A. Macdonald had a farm

Harry and Toronto	BOB ALDIS
Privatized Lives	DIANE SHEARS
Labattman	GLEN ACORN
"Meet Me in Saint-Louis-du-Ha! Ha!"	R.M. BAXTER
The Guess Who's Coming to Dinner	KURT HAGAN

Catch 35.2 (metric version)   GORD BRADY

The Chronicles of Sarnia   TIM HALE

Pair o' Toes Lost   PAUL TOTMAN

Joe Clark, Ha Ha Ha   THOMAS DEAN

Hudson's Baywatch   PETER MARUCCI

Who Framed Roger Abbott?   ENNO & JANA BUSSE

Tolkien's Trilogy: *The Fellowship of the Rink, The Two Peace Towers* and *The Return of Mackenzie King*
      BILL MACARTHUR

"Poutine on the Ritz"   DIANE BETHUNE

Plato's *Re: Public Works*   JIM YOUNG

A Brief History of Maclean's   TIM PENNER

CLEVER CLERIHEWS

The clerihew is a safe haven for all versifiers, even those whose metrical sense is so wonky they believe a metre is what you feed when parking. E. Clerihew Bentley (1875–1956), after whom the four-line verse form is named, required a rhyme scheme of AABB, but allowed the most ragged of metres. All the writer needs is a keen wit and the name of a well-known individual to toy with. Consider this gem by David Mayerovitch:

Kurt Browning
Has a fear of drowning.
That's why the life he's chosen
Is one where water's always frozen.

Or this one, from W.S. Gray:

Santa's wife
Leads a charmed life.
She vacations in Bimini
While he's stuck in a chimney.

The famous name may be dispensed with, as in Stuart J. Alcock's three responses to a call for clerihews about animals:

An armadillo
Makes a poor pillow
And its scales
Often snag the percales.

The ocelot
Is not
A household pet
Yet.

The noise of a purr
From a small ball of fur
Is the sound of a kitten
Emittin'.

The very fact of rhyming was fodder for M. Chapman:

Mr. Ebenezer Scrooge
Planned a prescient subterfuge:
He ordered goose instead of chickens
Just so it couldn't be rhymed with Dickens.

And for K.C. Angus:

In a clerihew about Cupid
I resolved not to use "stupid";
But it looks as though
I've done so.

Other clever clerihews:

Luciano Pavarotti
Went a little dotty
When they said he was gonna
Share the bill with Madonna.   PETER MARUCCI

Salvador Dalí
Found Rodin quite pally.
Henry Moore
Thought him a boor.   HELEN & TREVOR GILES

"I am weary," said Lucien Bouchard.
"I have clearly been working too hard.
If they call when I'm off on vacation
Say I'm busy dividing the nation."   JOE WALLACE

Said Vincent Van Gogh,
It sounds wrong, I know.
Brother Theo tends to scoff.
He prefers Van Gogh.   KEN PURVIS

Adam, said Eve,
I should like to conceive.
So it's up to you, dear.
You're the only guy here.   KEN PURVIS

The Three Kings
Might have taken nicer things
Than gold, frankincense and myrrh
Were.   JIM PARR

Charles Pachter
Was a vital factor
In the artistic use
Of moose.   JIM PARR

The talent of the crocodile
Is anything but versatile.
He is a giant saurian
Who won't fit into a DeLorean.   I.R. CAPEWELL

And this one, as the Japanese stock market lurched southward in 1997:

Prime Minister Hashimoto
Liked the odds of 6/49 Lotto.
Someone wins – he can't say
That about the Nikkei.

DAVID DUNSMUIR

Dr. Freud
Was annoyed
When my id
Hid.

RICHARD SAMUELSON

"Santa Claus – SHOO!"
Said Elizabeth Two.
"Skiing nude at Balmoral
Is just *too* immoral."

THOMAS M. DALY

Sir Isaac Newton
Must have been a cute 'un
To have the savvity
To theorize gravity.

HELEN LENNON

Marco Polo
Did not travel solo.
Something else he did not do, of course, is
Invent a game played with a ball, mallet and horses.

CHARLES CROCKFORD

Stephen Hawking
Isn't one for walking,
But in his mind can travel
To places where yours would unravel.

GEOFF OLSON

Ringo Starr
Plays drums, not guitar.
So there's no comparison
Between him and George Harrison.   SUE DULLEY

Socrates
Was very fond of cheese.
Other ancient Greeks preferred
Curd.   LOUISE RICH

Sam McGee
From Tennessee
Became the toast
Of a celebrity roast.   K.C. ANGUS

Keith Angus submitted that last one in 1993, just after the Progressive Conservatives were all but wiped out federally by the Liberals. He couldn't resist offering "a topical Tom Swifty: 'I was a PC candidate,' he said devotedly."

Harold Pinter
Doesn't like winter.
He finds in Santa Claus's
"Hohoho" a paucity of pauses.   KEN PURVIS

F. Scott Fitzgerald
With his reputation imperilled
Wrote wildly improbable tales
Of even improbabler males.   TIM ANDREW

Elizabeth Two,
Feeling decidedly blue,
Sighed, "Motherhood isn't much fun.
I envy Elizabeth One."   R.M. BAXTER

Condoleezza Rice
Always has to spell her name twice.
It isn't easy phoning for a pizza
When your name is Condoleezza.   NATALIA MAYER

Lucien Bouchard
Does not rhyme with "card," but with "car."
The English mispronunciation
Destroyed his faith in Confederation.

DAVID MAYEROVITCH

Felix Mendelssohn
Wrote hymns with his sandals on,
But he twanged his garters
When writing sonatas.   JIM PARR

Leonard Cohen turned pariah
At a singalong *Messiah*
When he warbled "Hallelujah"
More or less to the tune of "Johnny, I Hardly Knew Ya."

DAVID DUNSMUIR

Karen Kain,
En pointe again.
Is this her grand finale
Or should we start a tally?

Luciano Pavarotti
Once adored biscotti.
Now, to reach his upper register,
He settles for a tofu-veggie stir.

NORMA CRAWFORD & JOHN ILLINGWORTH

Mahatma Gandhi
Thought it really dandy,

Not to mention expedient,
To be civilly disobedient.   BARRIE COLLINS

Robin Hood
Was not all good,
But who would care if
He was but the sheriff?   PETER MARUCCI

Pope John Paul II
Is widely reckoned
A nicer man
Than Genghis Khan.   T.E.W. GOUGH

Mr. *Gough offered another clerihew in which fiddler Ashley MacIsaac "finds speed paradaisac." "I've put an extra* a *in* paradisac, *because I can't type; as there is no such word anyway, perhaps this doesn't matter."*

Babe Ruth
Could be uncouth.
Martin Luther
Was somewhat couther.   GARY E. MILLER

Lord Cholmondley
Pronounced words rumly;
If I'd his name
I think I'd do the same.   JIM PARR

John Keats sang about urns,
While Robbie Burns
Gave advice
To mice.   B.W. JACKSON

Henry James
Has two first names;

Gore Vidal
Has none at all.   ROBERT ROSEN

Machiavelli
Hasn't been on the telly.
No wonder *The Prince*
Fails to convince.   B.W. JACKSON

H. Rider Haggard
Was something of a blackguard
Who spent much of his time tippling
With Kipling.   MIKE SNIPPER & LESLEY P. LYON

Martha Stewart, femme fatale,
Eschews the banal.
Trouble is, she's total perfection
And we're all rather flawed in my cheering section.
                                                GORDON FINDLAY

Robert Milton
Learned that travellers wilt on
Learning their flight
Will depart the next night.   ALANNA LITTLE

Scarlett O'Hara
Of the plantation Tara
Loved her satins and silks
And, of course, Ashley Wilkes.   COLLEEN COULTER

Robert Browning
Was forever frowning,
Which is why it took him so long
To write "Pippa's Song."
                         MIKE SNIPPER & LESLEY P. LYON

The buffalo
Is rather slow
And can be confused with the bison
Even by a wise 'un.   ALANNA MATTHEW

The snowshoe hare
Winterizes with flair;
To make his coat blanch
He travels by avalanche.   ALANNA LITTLE

Frosty the Snowman
Tried to get a tan.
For Miami he set sail
And came back in a pail.   NORMAN F. GARVIN

before   after

Rudolph's claim
To lasting fame
Is hardly cause
For loud guffaws.   R.W. CROSBY

If only Bob Cratchit
Had wielded a hatchet
He might have done more
To even the score.   R.W. CROSBY

Though the rhinoceros
Is smaller than stegosaurus,
You may pay dearly
If you treat it cavalierly.   K.C. ANGUS

Good King Wenceslas
Cancelled the free repast
When he found the peasant
Had poached a royal pheasant.   JUNE ARDIEL

Katerina Witt
Every winter likes to flit
In filmy clothes around a rink.
She'd be much warmer in a mink.   BARRIE COLLINS

M r. Collins entered that one in 1993, long before the figure skater *doffed her duds entirely for a feature in* Playboy. *He also submitted this one:*

Santa Claus,
I'm told, abhors
(And I'm sure that you would too)
Seeing reindeer from his point of view.

S ince the beginning of the Challenge, perhaps to exercise their *muscles before engaging in the main event, a number of entrants have written verses about me. Flattering, no question. However, many seem to think my surname is stressed on the second syllable rather than the first. Margaret Howard got it right:*

Our challenger, Warren Clements,
Rewards all sorts of nonsense.
Specially silliness, whimsy and poesy.
Where other hacks fear to tread goes he.

I *n 1995, Lesley Hands Wilson took the precaution of putting my name in the middle of a clerihew line, where the issue would be moot:*

Warren Clements has quite the job
Controlling the Challengentsia mob.
I wonder, when he sits before his "Tuesday file,"
Does he smile?

A *nd, from Procter Le Mare:*

Warren Clements
Should do penance
For causing me to spend my time
Looking for a lousy rhyme.

M *r. Le Mare's real offering was this one:*

E. Clerihew Bentley's invention
Has advantages worthy of mention.
For one,
If it's hard to be brief when approaching the end you can
    just carry on till you're done.

HOLIDAYS FROM HELL

Among its other responsibilities, the Challenge makes a point of exorcising demons. If you have a terrible boss, you can transform the experience into a joke about the workplace. If you've been unlucky in love, you can reshape the misery into a boffo line about things you shouldn't have said on that first date.

In separate Challenges, readers were asked to suggest words that might signal caution in vacation-spot literature and to suggest lines you wouldn't want to hear on your vacation.

Chris Robbins wrote from New Brunswick to suggest the line "Usually this time of year the weather here is great." He explained: "Coming from a foggy town on the Nova Scotia coast, I have used this line myself on summer visitors who got stuck in a bad string of grey days. But I had the tables turned on me by the park ranger when tenting for a week near Vernon, B.C. It rained an awful lot for the near-desert conditions of the Okanagan Valley."

Among the unfortunate vacation brochures:

Anyone held hostage for more than thirty days receives a complimentary spa package.   GAIL GROSE

New, higher fences at the driving range!
We never run out of tranquillizer darts!

Free post-vacation counselling.
Still no sign of the Africanized bees!
Town Council has recently passed a 2:00 a.m. motorcycle
    curfew.   JOHN HARRIS

Dine by the romantic light of the flareoffs from the local
    refineries.
Our clothing-optional policy even extends to the kitchen
    staff.   COLIN EYSSEN

Now, cholera-free!!   STEVE MITCHELL

We think the war is over.
Now with 50-per-cent lower bribes expected.   TOM WITTE

Bathrooms are located conveniently close to the hotel.
                              PETER MARUCCI

The net around the bay keeps out all but the most deter-
    mined predators.
No need to bring a raincoat or an umbrella; we've got lots.
                              KEN PURVIS

Our private golf course has eighteen watchtowers.
                              BERT GASKELL

Receipts issued promptly for any confiscated personal effects.
Beaches are mine-swept regularly for your comfort and
    safety.   ALANNA LITTLE

Features twenty-four-hour Happy Hour.   B.W. JACKSON

You'll be pleased to note that we're constantly making
    improvements at our resort hotel.   BILL PLUMB

At the Oceanview Hotel we are proud to feature a telescope
  on every balcony.   AL WILKINSON

You will be very surprised by the hotel's proximity to the
  airport.   BARRIE COLLINS

Our friendly taxi drivers leave the meter off for tourists.
                                             NATALIA MAYER

Our guests tell us they can't wait to get out of our beds in
  the morning.   JOAN E. MARSHALL

And now, the remarks you would rather not hear on holiday:

"You're right. The brochure didn't mention that the total
  annual rainfall is all in this month."   C.N.R. STEWART

"Hey, you really do look like your passport picture."
                                             ANNABELLE DEGOUVEIA

"No, they aren't toy planes. They're mosquitoes."

RUHI E. TUZLAK

"Your room is 1205. The stairs are over there."

BERT GASKELL

"Are you here for the bikers' convention, or only on
vacation?" WILLIAM G. ALEXANDER

"If there is a microbiologist on board, could he please come
to the galley?"
"Didn't someone tell you about the civil war?"

COLIN EYSSEN

"Honey, this is the same town we passed through an hour
ago." J.T. CURRIE

"For the advertised convenient beach access, use bus
number 12." KURT LOEB

"Ordinarily all TVs and radios in the campground must be
off by eleven o'clock, but the owner's son just graduated
from high school and . . ." D.J. WELBOURN

"Of course it's Southern Ontario. For a lousy $399 you
expect the real London, Paris and Athens?"

BARRIE COLLINS

ADJUSTED FOR CANADA #1

Although most of the Challenges have been universal – the wider the canvas, the more potential targets or raw material – a number have concentrated on Canada.

A few were specific to events. When Canadian senator Andrew Thompson was suspended from the Senate without pay for his abysmal attendance record – he was living in Mexico – readers were asked to suggest possible excuses he might have had. For example:

He believes in the NAFTA life.   GORDON LEARY

He's concerned about John A. Macdonald's Revenge.
                                                  IAN BROWN

He sincerely thought he had been made a señor, not a
    senator.   FRANK HACHÉ

Then there was the challenge to name the new bridge between Prince Edward Island and New Brunswick, eventually called Confederation Bridge. Among the proposals:

Grilles in the Mist   ALANNA LITTLE

Bridge over Troubled Lobsters   HAYNES LEE

Charlottetown's Web   BRIAN E. DUCLOS

In honour of the two landing towns, Border and Cape
    Tormentine: BorderTorment Crossing
                                        LYNN BELLIVEAU

Readers were also asked to assume, for the sake of argument, that
Canada had a few shortcomings.

While others may have a super sex drive, Canadians have
    only a Sussex Drive.   KARL DILCHER

We are governed by Parliament, a word many believe was
    developed from two words from one of our founding
    nations: *parler* (to speak) and *mentir* (to lie).   J.T. CURRIE

If nuclear war breaks out on a Saturday night, Canadians
    won't hear about it until the end of the hockey game.
                                        PATRICIA TRIPP

Newfoundlanders have learned, since joining Canada, that
    "Confederation" is but an anagram of "cod-free nation."
                                        KURT LOEB

There was even a contest to adapt an old nursery rhyme to include
a reference to a Canadian place, person or institution. Call it "Mother
Canada Goose." Amanda Saper offered a page-long take on "The
Spider and the Fly," about The Tories and the Crowd – this being in
1993, at the nadir of the Progressive Conservatives' popularity. Brian
Mulroney had announced his resignation as prime minister but had
not yet been replaced by Kim Campbell. Sample lines:

"Our words will win you over with their logic and their
    truth.

98

Our speeches are designed to please the aged and the
    youth."
"Oh no," said the masses, "for we've often heard it said
They never live in happy times, who are by Tories led."

H *ere are four others:*

Revenue Canada, have you any wool?
Yes sir, yes sir, three bags full:
One for the wealthy, one for the wise,
And one to pull over the taxpayers' eyes.   K.C. ANGUS

The Bay of Fundy,
Tide-filled on Monday,
Fogbound on Tuesday,
Ice-choked on Wednesday,
Storm-tossed on Thursday,
Calm again on Friday,
Polluted on Saturday,
Fished-out on Sunday.
A week in the life
Of the Bay of Fundy.   PETER & DAWN MAITLAND

Ding-dong bell,
Brian's in the well.
Who put him in?
A big Canadian.
Who pulled him out?
Nobody.   LINDA KEMP

Mary had a bighorn sheep.
Its fleece was brown as gravel.
And everywhere that Mary went
That sheep was sure to travel.
It followed her from Calgary
Out west to Lake Louise.

And all the people laughed to see
A sheep on downhill skis.   SUE DULLEY

The most popular contests were those that fed popular expressions or famous sayings through a simultaneous-Canadian-translation machine. Peter Marucci was relieved in 1995, since the previous week's Challenge had been some exercise involving Thomas the Tank Engine. "You had me worried when the Challenge drifted off into children's stories about trains – a fairly limited field, I suggest – but now I'm more comfortable since it's back on a familiar (you should excuse the pun) track."

Wilma Riley, recalling the recent debacle over the failed Meech Lake constitutional accord, wrote in 1992, "Really, this seems too easy! I'm almost ashamed to send this in because it seems so obvious, but I am sending it anyway because it's so, well, Canadian. My entry for a Canadian twist to a common expression? 'Meech ado about nothing.' There, I did it. I'm just afraid I may not be the first."

Among the other Canadianized expressions and famous quotations:

You can't see the forest for the clearing.
Keep right on to the middle of the road.
Many dams make light work.
No sooner said than there's a Royal Commission.

JIM PARR

Hell hath no fury like a special interest scorned.

MORTON S. RAPP

The early bird gets to shovel the driveway.   AL WILKINSON

If at first you don't succeed, call another referendum.

A.C. STONE

Parliamentary, my dear Watson.   JAN TISSANDIER

She is a social blackfly.   CHARLES BATOMSKY

Moving at a mail's pace.   BARRY O'KEEFE

The longest journey begins with a single Via Rail lineup.

PETER MARUCCI

Fit as a fiddlehead.   GLENDA BOCKNEK

CN is believing.
There's no such thing as a free trade lunch.   NIGEL YONGE

Five o'clock shadow, 5:30 in Newfoundland.

AUDREY M. BATES

Rapunzel, Rapunzel, let down your trade barriers.

RUTH BROWN

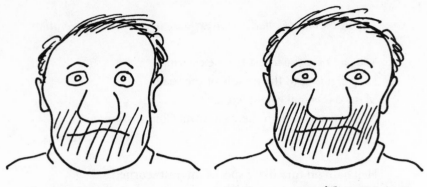

5 O'CLOCK SHADOW   5:30 IN NEWFOUNDLAND

Have a reasonably nice day.   K.C. ANGUS

Give me liberty or give me death, if it's not too much
    trouble.
Ask not what your country can do for you, ask what your
    province can do for you.

PENNY HOCKING & DAVID GARTRELL

Is that a registered pistol in your pocket or are you just
    happy to see me?   SYLVIA SIMPSON

I have appointed a commission to study the environmental
    and social impact of crossing the Rubicon.
The price of freedom is eternal vigilance plus GST plus PST.

PETER G. BARTA

If at first you don't succeed, apply for a Canada Council
    grant.
Ask a silly question, you're almost certainly in Parliament.

W.P. KINSELLA

Eat, drink and be merry and thank you for not smoking.

KATE COWAN

He who hesitates may have a point.   ALANNA LITTLE

Go for bronze!   TODD SHERIFF

Give me liberty or, at the very least, give me sovereignty-
association.   MARY LOU ROUTLEY

I came, I saw, I was just glad to have an opportunity to
participate.   JILL & ALEC MCCLAY

Nothing succeeds like in the U.S.   PAUL DAVY

He must be dreaming in beige.   PETER BERRY

Fifty-four forty or negotiate.   HELEN & PETER MARUCCI

Do unto others as you would have them do unto you if only
the money were there.   RON CHARACH

SECOND LINES

Sure, *it's easy to write the first line of a poem. You haven't reached the hard part yet: matching the metre, finding a rhyme, expanding the metaphor. This is where so many of our famous authors fall down. They start off well, and then it all falls apart one line later. "Ooh," you say to yourself, "what a nasty accident. If only somebody had been there to point them in a more rewarding direction."*

In 2001, the Challenge asked its readers to do just that, borrowing a leaf from Willard R. Espy's book Another Almanac of Words at Play. *Take a familiar line of poetry or song, we said, and add a second, rhyming line. The offerings poured in. Careful readers may notice that a couple of the opening lines were in fact the opening two lines of their original poems, but I have exercised editorial licence and waved them through.*

J.D.H. Iles, who urged the Challenge to run such a contest some time back, recalled the Sunday Observer *in Britain running a competition along these poetic lines in the 1930s. "I remember two entries: 'Silent upon a peak in Darien / I stayed for a week with my great-aunt Marian'; and, "'I drove the car, you read the map," the carping husband said, / "The night we went to Birmingham by way of Beachy Head.""'*

Helen Fogwill Porter, a professional writer, generally sends in her entries on postcards. The one for this contest was a promotional card for *Ed Kavanagh's* The Confessions of Nipper Mooney, *with a beautifully lit photograph of a boy gingerly holding a dragonfly in his cupped hands. This had nothing to do with the contest. I just thought I'd mention it.*

Allan Liggins prefaced his entries with this comment: "At last, a challenge to my vast knowledge of the most sophisticated and intellectual poetry of the English language." There followed variations on "Twinkle, Twinkle Little Star," "Little Bo Peep" and, reprinted below, "The Owl and the Pussycat."

The choice of a headline on the columns has always been my editor's. I have had a few editors, in particular Joan Danard early on and Jack Kirchhoff more recently, and have been lucky in them. As a rule, they reviewed each week's lineup for a phrase they could filch for the title – something that amused them, would fit the space, and would draw in the reader. For this challenge, Jack chose the second line from the poem about Miss Turner, and a lovely choice it was. I should mention that in 2001 Kathleen Turner was playing the role of Mrs. Robinson in a theatrical version of The Graduate, *in the course of which she had a brief and much-heralded nude scene.*

Once upon a midnight dreary,
My computer froze with a single query.   CHRIS CLARK

Hello, young lovers, wherever you are.
It's the police, so get out of the car.   C. DEL PINE

I have a little shadow that goes in and out with me.
I've charged it with harassment now I've got my law degree.
                                                  DEB CALDERON

Bring me my arrows of desire!
Viagra, too, in case I tire.   BARRIE COLLINS

My true love hath my heart and I have his.
The doc who did it really was a whiz.   G.D. WELLS

The stag at eve had drunk his fill
And whined at length about the bill.   ALANNA LITTLE

The moving finger writes, and having writ
Served on it, needs must quit.   K.C. ANGUS

The outlook wasn't brilliant for the Mudville nine that day.
Three players tested positive and weren't allowed to play.
GARY E. MILLER

Oft in the stilly night,
"Did I douse the downstairs light?"   FRANK H. GOUGH

Oft in the stilly night,
"Did I douse the downstairs light?"

To be or not to be?
The compromise: Reality TV.   JOSEPH E. DONNELLY

Lord, what fools these mortals be.
Except, of course, for you and me.   JUNE SKENE

My mistress' eyes are nothing like the sun.
They look somewhat like raisins in a bun.

WOLF KIRCHMEIR

The highwayman came riding, riding, riding,
Selling aluminum windows and siding.   PETER MARUCCI

I wandered lonely as a cloud,
Without directions (being too proud).   PATRICK GAGE

Then to the well-trod stage anon
To see Miss Turner sans chiffon.   FRED MOYES

The Assyrian came down like a wolf on the fold.
Was it terror or war? We were all Gallup-polled.

PADDY STAMP

The owl and the pussycat went to sea in a beautiful pea-
    green boat.
"Unusual case," the Canadian immigration officer wrote.

ALLAN LIGGINS

To see the world in a grain of sand
Requires a glass in the viewer's hand.   A. REDISH

The curfew tolls the knell of parting day.
Won't someone take that bloody bell away?

MARGARET WHITELEGG

In Xanadu did Kubla Khan a stately pleasure dome decree,
But now it's gone, because it had no waterproofing guarantee.

DEB CALDERON

We are the hollow men
Who shape the news at CNN.   JOHN MILLEN

Should auld acquaintance be forgot,
We'd save on Christmas cards – a lot.   JIM TEMPLETON

The storm came on before its time.
I went to bed with a gin and lime.

HELEN FOGWILL PORTER

The mirror cracked from side to side.
Prunella wasn't a lovely bride.   DON RECCHI

Stone walls do not a prison make.
Impair they do, a jailyard break.   CAMERON FRENCH

Let there be no moaning at the bar.
I only asked you for a pinot noir.   KEN PURVIS

'Twas brillig, and the slithy toves
Were served on toast from whole-wheat loaves.

KEN PURVIS

If I should die, think only this of me.
I've been on the waiting list since 1993.

BRENDAN J. O'BYRNE

THAT'S NOT WHAT I EXPECTED TO HEAR

Life *operates by such rigid rules. Suppose the rules were broken for a day, and people said what they never dared say, or, for the sheer orneriness of it, said the precise opposite of what they were expected to say. Suppose, as Tony Roberts wrote, that the Challenge editor explained the weekly judging of his contest this way: "My M.O.? Easy. Scatter entries on floor, press cat's paw on ink pad, then pirouette before tossing cat. The first ten paw-printed win."*

The assignment proceeded accordingly: Suggest a statement that is not what you'd expect to hear from someone engaged in a profession, craft or hobby. Alternative wording: Let's see how many shivers we can send up the spines of how many dedicated professionals and hobbyists. Karl Dilcher said he couldn't imagine any fictitious example being stranger than a Shakespearean actor reciting, "These are the voyages of the Starship Enterprise.*"*

Librarian: "I wanna hear some NOISE!"　　　CHRIS HURST

Arbitrator: "The best way of settling differences is a good old fist fight."　　　COLIN EYSSEN

Fishing guide: "Eeeeow! You're not sticking that poor worm on your hook, are you?"　　　GORDON FINDLAY

Lawyer: "Appeal? No, you win some, you lose some."

GARY E. MILLER

Undertaker: "Dead? They're supposed to be dead first?"

PETER MARUCCI

Priest: "You think that's a severe penance? Try being claustrophobic and having to listen to someone whose sins are as boring as yours for a few hours every week."

ERIC MENDELSOHN

Symphony orchestra conductor: "Okay, cats – wing it!"

GEOFF WILLIAMS

Food inspector: "How clean do these pots have to be? I mean, you're boiling things in 'em, ain't ya?"

RON CHARACH

Nutritionist: "Whose turn is it to bring doughnuts for our meeting?"

ALANNA LITTLE

School librarian: "Y'know, I think this literacy thing is way overrated." ELLEN GOLDFINCH

Dental hygienist: "Life is short, why waste time flossing?" GILLIAN BREEN

Bank inspector: "Okay, close enough." ERVIN STEMBOL

Famous painter, at the end of his Blue Period: "You mean this stuff comes in other colours?" MICHAEL WILKSHIRE

Philatelist: "Just lick 'em lightly on one corner, then they won't fall out of your album." JEAN E. SMYTHE

Surgeon: "I see that nobody marked which knee. Eeny, meenie, minie, mo. . . ." C.H. VANE-HUNT

Politician: "I moved here because I think you're the only people in the country stupid enough to elect me." CHARLES CROCKFORD

Baker: "These hypoallergenic cookies tasted blah, so I've added some peanuts and shrimp." PATRICK GAGE

Computer techie, to customer: "You wouldn't have a hammer I could borrow, would you?" CHRISTINE KEMP

Computer security expert: "If this is super-secret, how about we type the data on an old Remington and deliver the pages by hand?" GLEN ACORN

Model ship builder: "Hey, if you don't have the right smokestacks, send me anything ya got. It's only a toy, for cryin' out loud."

Gourmet chef: "It doesn't matter if you use fresh herbs or the old, dried-up stuff in the little jars. Who's gonna know?" JUDITH COTTRILL

Pedicurist: "What better job for a foot fetishist like me?" BARRIE COLLINS

Real estate agent: "I just showed you this place as a horrid example. You don't seriously want it?" K.C. ANGUS

ADJUSTED FOR CANADA #2

Sure, Champagne is Champagne and the Russian steppes are Russian. This, however, is a mere accident of geography. Any of the world's inventions, ideas or topographical features might as easily have emerged in Canada to keep company with the Rockies, Screech and poutine. There would just be a few subtle differences.

Sisyphus would be condemned to the endless task of
reinventing the CBC.　　　　　　　　　ALANNA LITTLE

Discerning palates would anxiously await Moosehead
Nouveau.　　　　　　　　　　　　　BARRIE COLLINS

The game of Monopoly would be called Jurisdiction.

L.J. KOH

Esperanto would have two official versions.

JOSEPH E. DONNELLY

Grey Cup tea.　　　　　　　　　　　COLIN EYSSEN

The Life-Without-Parole-for-Twenty-Five-Years Gardens of
Babylon.　　　　　　　　　　　　　ISAAC SOBOL

Grey Cup tea

The Venetian canals would have been filled in to provide
maximum condo development space.   BILL PLUMB

Discorde: the supersonic jet sponsored by Ottawa and
Quebec.   TONY CHANDLER

The Battle of Agincourt would probably have been lost
because of the cancellation of the arrow. FRANK MORGAN

Every federal action has an equal and opposite provincial
reaction.
The Spanish Armada would have been detained by the
Coast Guard.
The Charge of the Light Brigade was criticized by the
auditor-general.   K.C. ANGUS

Memo to interviewers for the position of Vestal Virgin: No
questions related to gender or sexual experience are
permitted.
The Tin Man is still waiting for his heart transplant.
Lacking an exemption from the Egg Marketing Board, the
Golden Goose had to lay the regular product.

DICK & SUE WATERMAN

Venus de Milo would have been discovered with an
   attached Canadarm.   JULIA HASTINGS & GERARD JEST

The Last Supper would have required a liquor licence.
   KARL DILCHER

The Labours of Hercules would involve community service.
The Ten Commandments would be the 1,426
   Recommendations.
Dom Perignon would make beer.   PETER MARUCCI

The Repeal of the Porn Laws.   JIM PARR

The Tower of Babel would be the National Centre for
   Multicultural Diversity.   S.F. SOMMERFELD

Storm Windows 98.   LOUIS DESJARDINS

The Big Bang would be a muffled gurgle so as not to annoy
   the neighbours.   STEPHEN DUDZIK

The Colossus of Rhodes would have been the Colossal Toll
   on Roads.   BRUCE MCFARLANE

The Ten Commandments would be in draft form, awaiting
   the report of the Royal Commission on Graven Images.
   DAVID DUNSMUIR

The Internet is launched by the government in Ottawa; five
   years later it has been used twice.
Environmentalists get wind of the Wright brothers' efforts
   on the Kitty Hawk dunes; the brothers are stopped cold.
   GORDON FINDLAY

All plays would begin with the lines, "How's it goin'?" "Not
   too bad."   ORLANDO MANTI

SHOPWORN TITLES

The Globe and Mail *may be an upmarket paper, and many of its readers may be upmarket, not to mention upright, upstanding and, except possibly late Saturday night, standing upright. The Challenge, however, does not play favourites, and is as comfortable with down-market literature as it is possible for an inanimate column to be.*

One of the Challenges in 2000, suggested by Ken Purvis, was to imagine that the themes or characters of famous works of fiction or non-fiction had been rewritten to be more shopworn or déclassé, and to suggest examples with helpful synopses. Kay S.L. Brant, who had just won another Challenge, prefaced her entries with a self-mocking cry: " 'Omigawd – She's back! Give her an inch and then watch out – another inundation of responses.' I guess that winning No. 405 (wow!) must have gone to my head or something."

Her entry was handwritten, a form that was more common when the Challenge started than it is in the age of unbridled e-mails. She appended a footnote: "As you can see, I'm still reduced to 'low-tech,' as everything post-Gutenberg remains in storage pending a few 'finishing touches' to our new quarters – like floors!" That explains one of her entries: "Who Has Seen the Window?: Someone mislaid one of the architectural drawings for our new home!"

As in so many other contests, it became clear that Challenge entrants would make excellent screenwriters. Steven Spielberg's attempt to update Peter Pan *in his film* Hook, *with Robin Williams as an older Pan who had to rediscover his inner child, could have benefited from a rewrite along the lines suggested by Barrie Collins:* "Peter Pot: An 'eternally' young hero ages, puts on weight and crashes into the orchestra pit when the wire breaks."

Indeed, David Crowe attached this notice to his paragraph-long reimagining of The Lord of the Rings: "Movie rights and product placement opportunities available." *His title was* Lord of the Rinse, *and the first sentence was this:* "A bored Maytag repairman is asked to repair, for the first time, a 1927 washing machine, leading him to start a global search for three replacement rings."

Jean Palmer didn't so much create an alternative version as deconstruct an existing one. "Tale of interfering little Victorian miss who harasses rabbits and caterpillars, uses flamingos and hedgehogs as croquet gear, nearly gets a poor cat beheaded and finally gets her comeuppance." *The title:* Malice in Wonderland.

Among other books that have fallen on hard times:

The Jingle Book. Mowgli, the wolf-boy, is reduced to writing lyrics for commercials after tiger-hunting is outlawed.

BARRIE COLLINS

The Bland Assassin. A killer bores his victims to death.

HELEN FOGWILL PORTER

The Parfait Storm. Frustrated fishermen have an intense, bitter argument over which kind of syrup to use for their dessert.

BILL PLUMB

The Story of Owe. A French courtesan goes heavily into debt.

GARY E. MILLER

The Remains of the Dinner. Stately home guests have to improvise breakfast when the staff goes on strike.

COLIN EYSSEN

the bland assassin

Bleeping Beauty. A pageant winner's foul language costs her
the title.
David Cop-a-Feel. An orphan grows up to be a sexual
predator.
Catsup in the Rye. On his first day tending bar, Holden
Caulfield tries to invent a new drink.

KAY & DONALD BRANT

Johnny Ragweed. Vagabond seed-sower goes down in
history as the bane of allergy sufferers.
The Just Because Stories. Rudyard Kipling's how-to book on
silencing annoyingly curious children.

KAT & NAT ROTHER

The Thirty-Nine Stops. Late to school and needing an
excuse, a boy blames the city bus.   PATRICK GAGE

The Way of All Flashers. One man's attempt to break the cycle of exhibitionism which has plagued his family for generations. LINDA LUMSDEN

The Book of Excuses. Moses explains to the Children of Israel why it took him forty years to find the way to the Promised Land, when it turned out to be really just a few sand dunes away. ZACHARY JACOBSON

Much I Do about Nothing: An employees' guide to appearing to be busy when there is no work to do. ALANNA LITTLE

The It-ching. A Confucian guide for eczema and dermatitis sufferers. DAVID GOLDBERG

David Chesterfield. An ambitious young man prepares for life as a couch potato. DAVID FRANK

Twelfth Knight, or What the Hell. King Arthur become frustrated with the steadily declining quality of applicants for seats at the Round Table. BILL KUMMER

How Tough a Neighbourhood Was It?

Welcome to the How section of the book. Johnny Carson was the most famous practitioner of the How joke. He would begin, "It was so cold . . ." The audience would shout, "How cold WAS it?" He would favour them with a half-smile and proceed to the joke: something along the lines of "It was so cold the refrigerator exchanged its light bulb for a heat lamp" or "It was so cold the ice cubes wore ear muffs."

Well, the Challenge knows a good routine when it spots one, so over the years the column has set a few How contests. This time round, the question was: "How tough was your neighbourhood?" The idea came from Globe colleague Jack Kapica, who in turn credited Jim Christy. The examples included: "It was so tough we used to steal hubcaps off moving cars."

Barrie Collins offered several entries, then went into a paragraph-long riff with the cadence of Rodney Dangerfield. "The girls pierced their ears with marlinspikes. Graffiti were written in blood. The funeral chapel had a conveyor belt. World War Two was where you went for R&R. We smoked unfiltered cigarettes. Canada separated from us. Anyone over twenty was considered a senior citizen. We thought Alcatraz was an island paradise. Hoo boy, we were tough!"

Hard to follow an act like that, but follow it we shall. For younger readers, the line about the prime minister is a reference to Jean Chrétien putting a chokehold on a protester in a crowd, which he later *referred to as a "Shawinigan handshake." Elsewhere, our neighbour-hood was so tough that:*

The cats went mousing in packs.
The police station paid protection money.
Bus service was provided by Brinks. K.C. ANGUS

The high-school metal detectors picked up fetal twins
wearing brass knuckles.
RANDAL & GREGORY MARLIN

The blood bank issued debit cards.
Wal-Pawn was the biggest store.
Only rich kids attended the school of hard knocks.
Learning penmanship had nothing to do with handwriting.
HERBERT P. WILSON

Parole was considered the family vacation.
LINDA LUMSDEN

Even atheists prayed when they came to visit.
The emergency ward at the hospital had an express line: ten
injuries or less.
We drank bottled water from Chernobyl Springs.
BRENDAN J. O'BYRNE

We used barbed wire to play tug-of-war. M. SANDERSON

The main street was called Jimmy Hoffa Avenue, after its
chief ingredient. R.T. RUGGLES

The politicians were afraid to lie to their constituents.
Kids played hopscotch with real Scotch. DOUG CHARLES

The brakes never squealed. TERRANCE D. SHEILS

Bank robbers got mugged while running to their getaway
  cars.   TAD FRANKLIN

The "Walk" light showed a running figure.   FRANK HACHÉ

"walk" sign in a tough neighbourhood

Kids had to be muzzled to protect the pit bulls.
                                                   B.W. JACKSON

The theatre popcorn booth sold boxes of unpopped
  kernels.   HELEN & PETER MARUCCI

Social status came from being a two-Uzi family.
                                                   COLIN EYSSEN

We weren't afraid to step in front of our prime minister
  when he walked through a crowd.

Our road-hockey league played on the Trans-Canada
    Highway.   CHARLES CROCKFORD

Baby booties were bronzed before they were worn.
                                     ELLEN BROWN

Generations of ducks swam on the water from the broken
    hydrant.   MARGARET TOTH

The ice-cream truck played Sid Vicious tunes.
We played hopscotch on the chalk outlines the police drew
    around the bodies.   RICK BOOK

The Avon lady sold pepper spray instead of hair spray.
                               NANCY BARCLAY

Neighbourhood Watch kept an eye out for the cops.
                          DOUG SUTHERLAND

The tune at the top of the charts was Taps.   FORBES HELEM

The church had stained-board windows.   CHRIS HURST

Loners travelled in pairs.
The firemen didn't make house calls.   JOE KEOGH

We used manhole covers as Frisbees.   MAURO NARDI

We made our Kool-Aid with Tabasco sauce.
                          JOAN E. MARSHALL

Baby rattles still had the snake attached.   R. WALLACE HALE

The teachers played hookey.   PAT MCALPINE

Make Mine a Job on the Rocks

As Scott Adams has shown in his comic strip "Dilbert" and the books based on it, the business world is a seething pit of incompetence, resentment, malice and sloth. This makes it perfect material for the Challenge.

Start with the job application. There is a right way to apply and a wrong way. Naturally, we were more interested in the wrong way. B.G. Markstad, who approved of this challenge, wrote, "When I was teaching my Grade 10s a few years ago how to make a résumé, I had them do a joke one and an interview as well as a serious one. The interviews were acted out in front of class and I haven't laughed so hard in years."

Wes de Shane recalled receiving "an application for a job we had advertised in the newspaper wherein the applicant said he had been very busy between jobs as he was 'suing his two previous employers for discrimination and wrongful dismissal.' He went on for three pages describing the allegations. Needless to say, we did not hire him."

Susan Athrens recalled that "in our first week in nursing school, we were asked why we had chosen nursing as a career. One woman responded: (1) helping people; (2) good pay; (3) easy access to drugs."

Here are other unfortunate things to say when applying for a job:

"What would a computer like that be worth on the street?"

GORD GATES

"As a crisis intervention mediator I've found that I can settle most disagreements with a good punch in the mouth."

WILLIAM M. VANCE

"Can the boss actually see the cash register from way up there?"

RON CHARACH

"Would you mind if I didn't wear my name tag? I don't really want anyone to know I work here." NIKKI PEARSON

"I think this business about washing hands before preparing food is just a conspiracy by big corporations to sell more chemicals."

BILL MACARTHUR

"How strict are your rules on theft and sexual harassment? Oh, I'm just curious, that's all."

DAVID CANN

"Should I happen to get pregnant, how much time off can I expect four months from now?"

BILL PLUMB

"The tremor tends to go away soon after my first surgical incision."

JOE WALLACE

"Security guard sounds pretty easy. It's not as if it's my own property."

K.C. ANGUS

"As a teller, do I have full access to the bank's vaults?"

GARY E. MILLER

"That's a picture of your daughter? Yowza!" JERRY KITICH

"I love this place. I used to shoplift here all the time."

MIKE ISACSON

"In my last job as a poker dealer, I liked to treat the gamblers at my table to some sleight of hand."   JANE HEYS

"Does Popular Music Publishers have a photocopier in the staff lounge?"   EDWARD BAXTER

All right. *Suppose you've landed the job against all the odds. Perhaps you didn't realize quite how tough it would be. Perhaps you're the elevator operator in the Tower of Babel (Michael Wilkshire), or the air traffic controller in an aviary (K.C. Angus), or a radio mime (Ken Purvis). You might be an orthodontist in Jurassic Park (C.H. Vane-Hunt), or Hannibal Lecter's nutritionist (Ron Charach) or a razor salesman in Neverland (Natalia Mayer).*

And, as with Dilbert, you might have a really dumb manager. Doug Haddow passed along "some gaffes from my late principal during the thirty-three years that I taught high school," including "In this office, we'll leave the status quo where it is" and "Anyone not hearing this P.A. announcement is asked to call the office immediately."

Others of that ilk:

"In purging files of obsolete documentation, please ensure that copies are made for the record."
"To avoid work disruption, the annual fire-safety evacuation will be conducted after office hours."

GORDON FINDLAY

"I've approved the Strategic Plan and the Mission Statement. Now, what are our goals?"   JIM PARR

"I know you've all been worked to the limit lately and it's not letting up, so I've brought in Joe. Who can show him around and train him for the next few weeks?"

FRANK HACHÉ

"No e-mails will be accepted without an original signature."

COLIN EYSSEN

Y *ou may find yourself searching for reading material to take your mind off the day-to-day grind, but don't look to the Challenge for help. A 1997 contest asked readers to suggest ways in which titles of books, movies and plays might be adjusted to reflect hiring and firing in the 1990s. Here are a few of the best:*

Now We Are Six, Doing the Work of Twelve.

MAUREEN KORMAN

Exit, Us.

ALYSSA DIAMOND

Watership Downsized.

JENNIFER AMEY

Honey, I Shrunk the Paycheque.

HELEN & PETER MARUCCI

The Importance of Being Earners.
Beyond the Fringe Benefits.

GEOFFREY PIERPOINT

Exit Interview With the Vampire.

MARK HANSON

All Quit on the Western Front.

ERIC KOSKY

The Head Count of Monte Cristo.

ALANNA LITTLE

Fifth Business Failure.

ROBERTA BAIRD

Juno and the Paycut.

NORMA CRAWFORD & JOHN ILLINGWORTH

Are You Being Severed?

M. SANDERSON

Boom, Bust and Hello, I'm a Consultant.

RICK BOOK

On a Clear-Out-Your-Desk Day You Can See Forever.

K.C. ANGUS

Then, *one day, you get the feeling your job is insecure. One reader suggested one of the warning signs – "You attend the weekly Section Heads meeting and find your name and Section are no longer on the Organization Chart" – and added: "The above is a true story. I went to a Section Head meeting as usual. We were all handed a copy of the new organization chart and I found my Section had been eliminated. Needless to say, I broke the news to the rest of my Section in a more appropriate manner."*

Here are other signs your job may be on the rocks:

The name on your doorplate is a Post-It note.

PETER MARUCCI

In lieu of a Christmas bonus, your boss gives you a gift-wrapped Squeegee.

SCOTT LEE

Your company physical is scheduled with Dr. Kevorkian.

LOLITA WIESNER

Your computer no longer asks you if you want to save your documents.

DANIEL TISCH

- You are put on straight commission, and your job has nothing to do with sales.

RON CHARACH

Your immediate supervisor is replaced by a chimp.

DOUGLAS R. MAH

Your name has been erased from Minesweeper's best times.
Your militantly feminist secretary asks if she can make you coffee.

BARRIE COLLINS

Your stationery requisition for twenty staples is rejected as excessive.

COLIN EYSSEN

Your boss wants you to show his son "whatever you do here." CHRISTINE SRI

Management installs a revolving door to your office.
Your co-workers snicker uncontrollably whenever you bring up the subject of career planning.
Your CEO is moonlighting at McDonald's.
JEFFREY S. MORRY

Your screen saver is an application for employment insurance. PAUL DAVY

There's a photo of a strange family on your desk.
GEOFF WILLIAMS

Your elevator access card will only take you down.
All employees get new passwords, and yours is "takahike."
CATHY GILDINER

When a new employee asks if you are from Helsinki, he explains that he was told you were Finnish.
BRIAN YAMASHITA

The company hands out calendars one month at a time.
A wrecking ball keeps interrupting your staff meeting.

BRENDAN J. O'BYRNE

A delivery person asks you politely not to sign the waybills.

MIKE CARROCETTO

Your boss hides under his desk each time he hears a police
siren.

KARL DILCHER

People are evasive when you ask, "What's new?"

MARGARET TOTH

Your business-trip plane ticket is one-way.
The office boy throws your mail in from the doorway.

BERT GASKELL

Your boss asks you how to spell "redundant."

PETER SMITH & KATIE ANDREWS-SMITH

Your new cubicle has a urinal and a sink.   JEAN SORENSEN

The office wall hangings are moving blankets.

MARK HANSON

S *till, let us not assume the worst. Let us assume you manage to
stick with the job for a while longer, and then have to leave. Terence
Walsh, who suggested this Challenge, set the scene this way: "Everyone knows you have been fired for your particular personality flaw.
But to avoid being sued, the company disguises it and even throws a
party for you. What oblique acknowledgment do you make in your
gift-acceptance speech?"*

"In retrospect, I would have advised that we attempt to go
paperless rather than try to bribe the fire marshal."

"I regret that the many bottles of Scope I've been receiving anonymously over the years were not coming from the same deranged individual." RON CHARACH

"Now I'll have time to visit the places my expense account says I've already been to."
"I guess I'll have to take credit for that. I've taken credit for everything else." CHARLES CROCKFORD

"A string bikini was perhaps carrying the concept of casual day too far." COLIN EYSSEN

"Incidentally, I would hope that spittoons will indeed become standard office furniture in the near future."
"It has yet to be satisfactorily explained to me why pet dogs are allowed in the workplace, but not pet goats."
BILL PLUMB

"It was foolish of me to have boasted about our secret offshore funds at the tax inspectors' ball."
"I should have thought twice about subletting my office on weekends." JOHN O'BYRNE

"I'd like to thank management for giving me the time, among other things, to start my own office-supply company." HELEN & PETER MARUCCI

"And I know that having the desk farthest from the washroom is not an excuse." PAUL DAVY

REJECTION LETTERS

W hat could be funnier than rejection? Rejection of the famous, of course. With that in mind, and conscious of the extensive literary knowledge of the readers, the Challenge asked for rejection letters that might have been received by famous authors, current and past.

Frederick Harrison provided several possibilities, and ended by saying, "I am tempted to put down a few more, but discretion tells me that the quality of any future results is likely to diminish quite precipitously." Charles Crockford imagined that+ a Canadian publisher would tell Charles Dickens that "we will not consider A Tale of Two Cities *unless you change the setting to Medicine Hat and Moose Jaw,*" to which Mr. Crockford added: "Just couldn't resist. I'm originally from 'the Hat'!"

Incidentally, the Challenge column, far from receiving a rejection letter, was invited into the pages of Reader's Digest *in March 1995. The magazine printed a few excerpts from a contest that had appeared the previous year in which readers were asked to create a corporate name by combining two or more existing corporate names. Among them were three by the winner of that contest, William M. Gulycz. (1) 3M, Goodyear: mmmGood. (2) John Deere, Abitibi-Price: DeereAbi; (3) Playboy, Toys 'R' Us: Boy Toy.*

Ken Purvis, one of whose lines the Digest *included, commemorated the occasion with a poem:*

Digest *contributor Purvis*
Is getting somewhat nervous.
Will he now become an admirer
Of the National Enquirer?

Certainly we had better luck than these authors:

To Ray Bradbury re. *Fahrenheit 451*: You are right, that's the
    exact temperature that paper burns at. Coincidentally,
    we are unable to return your manuscript.

JERRY KITICH

Dear John: We are currently considering three other
    Gospels, by Matthew, Mark and Luke, and do not need
    another at this time.   R.J. OLAJOS

By the end of your collected dialogues, Mr. Plato, we found it
    a little predictable that Socrates always wins the argument.

JOHN ROWELL

Dear Mr. Heller: We are returning *Catch-22* because we do
    not publish first novels. However, if it isn't your first
    novel, we still can't publish it because you previously
    used another publisher.   LINDA LUMSDEN

Dear Mr. Solzhenitsyn: Regretfully we return *The Gulag
    Archipelago.* Since you don't seem very keen on the place,
    we doubt it will persuade our readers to visit. Yours,
    World Wide Travel Guides.   CLIFF MCCAWLEY

Dear Mr. Shakespeare: We are returning *As You Like It* and
    Much Ado About Nothing. We didn't and it was.

STEWART FISHER

Dear Mr. Alighieri: We are returning your comedy manuscript, as we are a serious publisher and not into funny books. B.W. JACKSON

Dear Mr. Eliot: We are returning *Middlemarch* because we feel the subject matter would be better handled by a woman. CHARLES CROCKFORD

Dear Mr. London: Your dog stories, while delightful, would be even more so were the animals to converse with their human companions. BRUCE W. ALTER

Dear Mr. West: We regret to inform you that the editor's dog has chewed up *The Shoes of the Fisherman*. KEN PURVIS

From *Reader's Digest* to Stephen Hawking re. *A Brief History of Time*: Not brief enough for our purposes, I'm afraid. Better luck elsewhere. FREDERICK HARRISON

We will not publish this, Dr. Seuss
Do not resubmit, there is no use.
We will not publish this at our firm.
We will not publish, it makes us squirm. CHRIS HURST

Dear Mr. Almighty: Like many first efforts, Genesis is marred by sensationalism and gratuitous violence. JULIA GOTZ

Dear Mr. Shakespeare: "Shall I compare thee to a summer's day." In our climate? Rejection. COLIN EYSSEN

Dear Mr. Joyce: We are, like, sorry, but we're returning your manuscript *Ulysses*. Needs more, like, action, you know? Also, sentences are too long. PHIL PYE

To Charles Dickens, re. *A Christmas Carol*: We were going to publish your manuscript, but then we had visions of the three spirits of red ink, bankruptcy and foreclosure.

JERRY KITICH

Dear Mr. Chaucer: Your *Tales* appear a curious mixture of English and French. You might try the Canadian government as a publisher.   FRANK W. MORGAN

Dear Mr. Webster: We are returning your manuscript as it is too wordy.

Dear Mr. Roget: We are returning your manuscript as it is too wordy, verbose, long-winded.   JANET ZEMAITIS

Dear Sirs: I loved the central character – very *sympathique*. Try working on the title. The Holy Bible just isn't marketable. And oh! that ending. We might be able to do a serialization, and could start with Revelations as an attention-getter. There is definitely some good stuff in there, but the numbering system has to go. Get back to us.

GEOFF WILLIAMS

To Mr. Ogden Nash:
Your tendency to make up words
We find quite irritating.
Because of this, your poetry
We won't be "publicating."   SETH BROWN

Dear Mr. Tolstoy: Be advised that we will not be publishing your novel *War and Peace*. Nor will we be returning the manuscript, which was destroyed when it was dropped by the delivery boy and fell through three complete floors of our building, killing two employees on the way down. May we suggest an editor for your next project?

PAULA LANGE

Dear Mr. Homer: We're sorry, but we cannot publish *The Iliad* until you tell us your last name.   DEXTER HIGGINS

rejected   very rejected   thoroughly rejected   irretrievably rejected

SKEW THAT PROVERB

If *you half-recall a famous quotation but can't remember who said it or where to begin looking for it, the trick is to fall back on a weasel phrase. The language is full of them, and they permit casual paraphrases of thoughts that may once have been expressed by somebody famous enough to bother citing. "As a wise person once said . . ." "As the old saying goes . . ." "To quote a memorable phrase . . ."*

The Challenge has gone one better. Not content with the aphorisms and proverbs as originally constructed, we have reworked them to our liking. In 1993, the contest was to "amend an aphorism to alter its meaning." In 1998, the more elaborate assignment was to "invert or otherwise modify a proverb to reverse, alter or pervert its meaning." The amended versions frequently outshone the originals, although a few old favourites (read: I've heard that one before) showed up in the mailbag, such as the line "Time wounds all heels."

Molly M'Gillis wrote: "Here is Psalm 23 according to one of my students: 'The Lord is my Shepherd. I need everything I have.' It was almost as good as the day I heard about the Dead Sea Squirrels."

Whoever toys with the most gins dies.
Eternal dalliance is the prize of puberty.
He who laughs last probably didn't get it.

MAUREEN KORMAN

137

Mother has the necessity of intervention.
Life begins at party.
The end justifies the jeans. MARGARET MACNEILL

A bird in the hand is a damn nuisance. B.W. JACKSON

The uneasy head that wears the crown lies.
TONY CHANDLER

You can't judge a crook by his cover-up. ANDREW WEEKS

Don't count your mittens before they're matched.
The early Bard gets the words.
NORMA CRAWFORD & JOHN ILLINGWORTH

Boys will be noise. BARRIE COLLINS

It is natural to abhor vacuuming.
Bedfellows make strange politics. LESLEY HANDS WILSON

Accents make the hair grow blonder.
Where there's second-hand smoke there's ire. KEN PURVIS

You do not know a man until you've walked away with his
shoes. PAUL GOTTLIEB

Red sky at night, something's alight.
It is better to arrive than to travel economy. COLIN EYSSEN

The goose is good for the gander.
No bad deed shall go unpublished. KEVIN MELLEMA

Many hands would like work.
A fool and his money are soon partying.
Factions speak louder than works. BRENDAN J. O'BYRNE

Beauty is in the eye of the beer holder. CORNELL ATKIN

He who palpitates has lust.
Marry in haste, repeat at leisure. PAUL KOCAK

People who live in White Houses shouldn't tap phones.
CHERYL MINUK

It's better to have loved and won than to go through the
whole damn thing again. PETER DEAS

Duty is in the eye of the beholden. BETTY M. WOLFF

He who marinates is sauced. JULIE RUSH

Absinthe makes the fond grow hearty. JOHN O'BYRNE

He who hesitates is bossed.
If you aren't part of the solution, you're part of the
government.
Only the young die good. PETER MARUCCI

Old whines in new quibbles. RON CHARACH

Don't throw out the Bubba with the Whitewater.
We all have our crotches to bare. DAVID GIUFFRIDA

A friend in need is a friend to avoid.
Home is where the harm is. K.C. ANGUS

The road to the Hill is paved with good pretensions.
JIM PARR

A man is known by the company he downsizes.
Gather neuroses while ye may. ALANNA LITTLE

gather neuroses while ye may.

The bigger they are, the more likely you'll share your train
seat with their parcels.　　　　ALANNA LITTLE

You can't judge a book by the movie.　　　ROBERTA BAIRD

If you can't beat 'em, why join 'em?
You can lead a horse to water, but you won't want a drink
once he's been in it.　　　DOROTHEA HELMS

He who laughs, lasts.　　　　KURT LOEB

He who laughs last and best is picked for a comedy
program studio audience.　　　R.A. RAMSAY

What grows up must calm down.　　　THEA GRAY

Honesty is the best fallacy.　　　BETTY M. WOLFF

He who agitates is tossed.　　　TOM FISHWICK

Familiarity breeds intent.
Affluence makes the heart grow fonder.　　　FAY TEPPER

He who pays the piper pays the GST.　　　R.H. SQUIRES

MEANINGLESS MAXIMS

Think of the sayings that follow as the placebos of aphorisms. They have no nutritive value, but they sound awfully wise until examined more closely.

The Challenge was to write meaningless maxims, and for the most part meaningless is what I got. "As if there weren't enough pointless maxims around," wrote Peter Marucci, "you want more! Well, okay." Noel Wagner wrote, "Your challenge recalls one I heard years ago which went as follows: 'A rolling stone gathers momentum.'"

If there was any problem with the contest, it was that many of the entries were thoughtful, even profound – which didn't fit the assignment. Saying something without saying anything is an art. Politicians make it seem easy, but it's not.

Other aphorisms to live by:

It's a long road that has no end to it.   DAVID DUNSMUIR

Even those in short sleeves may reach for the stars.

PAUL DAVY

It is a lucky man who is blessed with good fortune.

PETER BRODIE

Behold the turtle: Upside-down, he faces the sky.

GEORGE DUNBAR

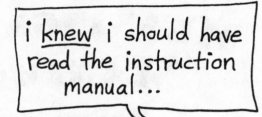

A bigger pail will hold more water.

HELEN & PETER MARUCCI

Forty clocks strike the same hour as four hundred.

S. LAMBERT

The rose also wilts for the hermit.   JEFFREY PERKINS

The can opener only goes round the can once.

BRENDAN J. O'BYRNE

Two's company, but one's indivisible.   JIM PARR

As ye sew, so shall ye repair.   PAUL DUNSEATH

An abandoned building is still full of air.   LES HOLROYD

Blood is thinner than porridge. BARRIE COLLINS

It's great to be great, but it's far, far greater to be greater.

RON CHARACH

An electric blanket can warm cold feet.
A bird on the wing will soon be gone. CRAIG SWICK

Many words make long books.
He who gives up his seat, stands. MARTIN CRISTOPHER

Washington and Moscow can never be in the same time
zone. KURT LOEB

The higher the aim, the greater the angle.

HELEN & TREVOR GILES

The answer depends on the question. CHRISTINE SRI

Thunder is the bellwether of rain. IAN BROWN

You can make any object smaller by merely decreasing its
size. HENRY G. SETO

SIN CITY

The Challenge has more on its mind than entertainment. It seeks to fill inexplicable holes in the language and the culture. Consider sin. Once you have worked your way through the seven deadly ones and a few mildly discomfiting ones, you have exhausted the works.

The Challenge, then, was to suggest and briefly explain new sins that might be added to the catalogue. The idea was submitted by artist Irma Coucill, who asked, "Are there more sins committed in this new century because of technology and changing lifestyles?" She suggested blastphemy (playing car radios too loud), gindulgence (excessive intake of martinis) and cignorance (smoking in a restricted area).

After the Challenge ran she wrote to say she had enjoyed the list, and was particularly surprised by "the far-flung addresses of your respondents." The contributors that week stretched in Canada from British Columbia to Nova Scotia. They wrote in from Brno in the Czech Republic (Karl Dilcher was on vacation there), England, Ireland and the United States. Paul Holland of Bognor Regis said he had heard of the Challenge through the British newspaper the Independent, which runs a similar competition.

The geographical mix was by accident rather than design, since I judge the entries without reference to name or address of author. Even addresses I would have longed to include in other weeks – in Singapore, China, Costa Rica, in periods when the column was top-heavy with

Toronto and Ottawa – haven't made the cut if they weren't attached to a good joke. The same goes for famous writers, though I recall the happy day when W.P. Kinsella submitted entries which more than made the grade. Having grown up on the music of the Lovin' Spoonful, I was similarly chuffed when an entry arrived from former member Zal Yanovsky, who was by then running a restaurant in Kingston and had a knack for this stuff. He entered a few times and was the winner one week.

In other words, while I have worked to avoid the sin of celebrity worship, I have sometimes been able to have my cake and eat it, too. And speaking of sins, here is an attractive assortment to choose from, should you be tired of virtue and in the market for something a little more thrilling.

Jane Langille offered an amusing acronym for the sins: Peglaws, for pride, envy, gluttony, lechery, avarice, wrath and sloth. Tony McCoy O'Grady wrote from Dublin, "Original Sin has been redefined as stealing an Apple iMac." Terry Monks wrote from Saskatoon, "The most heinous new sin is that of cellfishness, as displayed by the twits who come into my favourite coffee shop and talk far too loudly on their cellphones while I am trying to read my Globe and Mail."

Skillduggery: Padding of résumés.
Queuepidity: Stealing someone's place in the line.
Obviouscation: Making boring conversation.
Chrétienity: Professing belief in a natural ruling party.

JOHN MAYHOOD

Humicide: Murdering a tune.   DAVID CROWE

E-dultery: Chatroom infidelity.
Effrontery: Dependence on the f-word in conversation.

JOE DONNELLY

Bearing false wittiness: A comic's act of passing off a joke
    writer's work as his spontaneous humour.

GARY E. MILLER

humicide

Architorture: Inflicting hideous and insensitive alterations
on historic or otherwise pleasing buildings.

EDWARD SMITH

Provanity: Swearing at oneself in the mirror.

CHRIS GOSLING

T-4nication: Sleeping with your tax auditor.

KARL DILCHER

Pide: A high, overbearing opinion of one's pastry.

JANE LANGILLE

Prid: Being too arrogant to spell-check. PAUL HOLLAND

Barbiedollatry: The worship of the unattainable figure.

CALUM MACFARLANE

Animal crewelty: Dressing one's pets in homemade
    sweaters.   MEG SULLIVAN

Robery: Stealing bath accessories from a hotel.
Joywalking: Being a pedestrian among gridlocked cars.
Bridery: Paying money to have a bouquet thrown at you.
                      COLIN STANDFIELD

Statulence: Emitting spurts of disconnected figures as
    though they were convincing arguments.
Newmoania: "I gotta have a new [computer, SUV, BMW etc.]."
                      ZACHARY JACOBSON

Fidolatry: Pampering the dog.   B.W. JACKSON

Perseversion: Sticking to that strange habit no matter what.
Denvy: The neighbours have a larger family room than you.
                      COLIN EYSSEN

Bleakmail: Distributing depressing e-mail accounts of one's
    latest symptoms.   KEN PURVIS

Rvy: Envying thy neighbour's Winnebago.
                      GRAEME FOSTER

Carrogance: Sports-car owners' attitude to speed limits.
Bustfulness: The pride that goeth after implants.
                      AL WILKINSON

Emineminence: The triumph of notorious rap stars over
    the forces of good.   A.K. WALSH

Original sinema: Daring to see a movie before reading a
    published critic's review of that movie.   BRUCE COTE

Javarice: Excessive intake of coffee.   J.T. CURRIE

Slowth: Crawling along in the fast lane.   TONY CHANDLER

Incollarance: An unreasoning hatred of casual Fridays.
Lapathy: A studied indifference to exotic dancers.
                                                BARRIE COLLINS

Duvetousness: Longing for one's partner's bed covering.
AT&Theism: Worship of your Internet provider.
Jellocy: Preferring your child's dessert to your own.
                                        TONY MCCOY O'GRADY

Mallevolence: Pushy, boorish behaviour in crowded
    shopping areas.   TOM WITTE

Rignorance: Stomping on the brakes when you are being
    tailgated by a Mack truck.   ROB FREEMAN

Mastercide: A clone killing his original to obtain his inheri-
    tance and his life.   BOB CUMMING

Diskussing: Using strong language when the computer
    crashes.   MARILYN PENNER

THIS SPORTING LIFE

T o me, the world of sports is like the planet Mars. I know it's there, everyone talks about it, and I could probably see it with the right equipment, but that's as far as it goes. I clue in when people talk about the World Cup (the competitors are known by the names of their countries rather than of teams that keep getting sold to other cities) and I know the principle of the games, but if I were to set a Challenge devoted to the specifics of sports I would have to ask someone else to judge it.

Still, nothing ventured, nothing fumbled. In 1996, Charles Crockford suggested asking how you know a sports team is having a bad day, and offered this example: The coach has somebody else's name on the back of his jacket. The entries flooded in.

They change the team motto to "Let's play for fun!"
They go for drinks *before* the game.   NEIL MURPHY

The Booster Club has an unlisted phone number.
The team mascot wears his street clothes during the game.
Game results are listed under "Casualties" in the newspaper.
The team's song is "The Sound of Silence."   JAN WARREN

The newspapers send cartoonists instead of photographers.

BERT GASKELL

The owner demands to be traded.   BARRIE COLLINS

Hockey fans give standing ovations for shots on goal.

ARTHUR LOUIE

The team's only sponsor is a funeral director.
Marcel Marceau has been named team cheerleader.

LES HOLROYD

The team mascot has been barbecued for the sports
    celebrities' dinner.   KURT LOEB

The scalpers make more money recycling tickets than
    selling them.   RYAN PENNER

Your goalie has a sunburned neck from the red goal light.

SHAWN WHITE

The team sponsors are Butterfinger and Snickers bars.
The scoreboard clock has a snooze alarm.
The play-by-play commentary is pre-recorded.

ALANNA LITTLE

The owner wins the Marg Schott Humanitarian of the Year
    award.   DONALD M. WHITE

The CBC pre-empts the game to show the national newscast.

JONATHAN DANIELS

The huddle gives the quarterback claustrophobia.

B.W. JACKSON

The ice at your opponent's end never needs flooding.

WENDY WARNOCK

Team members pester loyal fans for autographs.
Balls hit into the stands are thrown back.   TOM MCGUIRK

Photos of your opposition are prominent on your grand-
    mother's mantle.   DOUG MOUNCEY

The souvenir booth doesn't carry any home apparel.

MARILYN PENNER

The crowd chants "Go, team, go!" when the owner threat-
    ens to move the franchise.   ANPAN YOSHIDA

The batting-practice pitcher leads the team in strikeouts.

MIKE MCCALLUM

The crowd calls a time-out.
The cheerleaders misspell the team's name.

GARY E. MILLER

The team gives ticket refunds on fan appreciation night.

JIM MOORE

The team mascot is roadkill.
The visiting team doesn't show up and the home team still
    loses.
The players refer to things like a "football net" and a
    "hockey bat."
The players are watching another game on portable TV sets.

PETER MARUCCI

They release only the negative of their team picture.

ROBERTA BAIRD

The team schedules its home games away.

GORDON TERNOWETSKY

The sportscasters use voice scramblers.

ANNIE & ROWAN MASSEY

Encouraged by the response to that contest, I arranged a couple of others. Since talk of the Olympics was in the air in July 2001 (until Toronto lost its bid to host the 2008 Summer Games), the assignment was to suggest simple amendments to real sporting competitions – whether or not they were part of the Olympics – to add a new element of interest. For example, the horseshoe toss: Shoes must remain attached to the horses.

A great many readers suggested playing water polo with horses, and a couple suggested a great sport that had, alas, been used as an example in an earlier Challenge: the javelin catch. In fact, Barrie Collins wrote to say, "I just found your 'javelin catcher' reference from last week in a 1981 paperback called Henny Youngman's 500 All-Time Greatest One-Liners, and I'll bet it was old long before then."

Here are a few amended sporting competitions, with a brief description of the rules:

Russian lawn bowling: Every sixth ball explodes on impact with the grass.

DAVID CROWE

The caber toss: Contestants must replant their trees.

DAVID ANTSCHERL

Bowling with bodychecking.
Ice-fishing in the middle of a hockey game.

NATALIA MAYER & DEREK SMITH

Calf-roping: To take place in conjunction with the three-legged race. Subjects must remain tied for the race's duration.

ROSALIND COOPER-KEY

Show jumping: To meet Humane Society requirements, riders have to carry the horses over the jumps.

COLIN EYSSEN

Downhill skiing: All the entrants start at the same time.

GEOFF WILLIAMS

Synchronized swimming: Must be accompanied by atonal music.

BRUCE W. ALTER

Hundred-yard dash: The yards will be separated by picket fences.

PUDGE MCDIVITT

The 440-metre cumulative relay race: Instead of passing a baton, the winner of the first lap leaps onto the back of the next runner, and so on.

SYD CLAY

Synchronized diving: Divers must avoid crowd of synchronized swimmers in the pool below.

DESI CHAMBERS

Curling: Players use vacuum cleaners instead of brooms.

CHARLES CROCKFORD

Running for men and women: In high heels.

ODETTE MEURER

S_till, no sport is so difficult that a committed athlete can't find a way to cut a few corners. In 2002, inspired by a recent survey that found 82 per cent of U.S. senior executives admitted cheating at golf, I asked readers how you can tell that someone is cheating at a sport or game._

Geoff Williams wrote: "There have actually been some intriguing efforts at high-level cheating in sports. I recall a European champion discus-thrower who was disqualified because somebody noticed that as his discus was in flight a piece fell off it, allowing it to become lighter. In a championship table-tennis match many years ago, a player was found to have a device that inflated and deflated the blade of his bat during play."

Other signs of cheating:

After a hotly contested game of checkers, you notice that
    two of your opponent's buttons are missing.

DOROTHY CHARACH

The referee is wearing the same shirt as the home team.

GEOFF WILLIAMS

Dance marathon: She is attached to the rafters with puppet
    strings.
Triathlon: Triplet brothers enter under one name.

PETER BIRRELL

The "woodchuck" that dropped your golfing buddy's ball
    into the hole comes running up to him for a treat.
The marathon winner drops his bus transfer.   TERRY REID

Bridge: The partners wear shin pads.   TOM BATCHELOR

Golf: His "ball" is in contact with air-traffic control.

JOHN O'BYRNE

The coach has the kids fingerpainting with pine tar before
the Little League baseball game. CAM FRENCH

Musical chairs: Thumb tacks. RODNEY SCANSEN

Checkers: He castles.
Poker: He wins. SETH BROWN

Darts: Your opponent doesn't drink six pints before the
match. JANE HEYS

Discus: The name Wham-O is lightly stamped in the
centre. STEPHEN DUDZIK

To a friendly game of Monopoly, he brings his real estate
agent. DARRYLL DOUCETTE

TUNE SALAD

The Challenge tries to appeal to a broad cross-section of readers, young and old. This seems to me the only way to operate a general-interest column: to assume that interests transcend age brackets, and that, for instance, a sports reference may whiz by people who don't follow sports (see previous chapter) but will amuse the twenty-five-year-old fan and the seventy-five-year-old fan alike.

Sometimes this conceit gets a mite tricky. Consider song titles. Unlike old movies, which appear regularly on television, and classic books, which cross most people's paths at some point in school, songs are not common currency. Radio stations hive off their audiences. The lover of Broadway shows may have no opportunity, let alone desire, to learn what rock fans hold dear.

As a result, sometimes I am blindsided. For instance, the Challenge asked readers to imagine song titles that didn't quite make it. One of the examples offered was "Fool Halfway Up the Hill," which I imagined everyone would recognize as a play on the Beatles' "Fool on the Hill." I received this note from an older entrant whose wit I knew to be sharp and whose range I had found to be broad. "I am disheartened. I spent the weekend trying to connect 'Fool Halfway Up the Hill' to any song I know. I can't. Perhaps it is the one-day smash hit of last week's superstar; that would account for it. Say – hasn't anything to do with Teddy Roosevelt? Or Jack and Jill?"

While the Beatles figured in several entries to that contest – the Luther Holtons offered "She Came to Clean the Bathroom Window" as their also-ran title – the recognition gap was sobering. I have tended to err on the side of the very famous in the song challenges, while occasionally tossing in more obscure titles for flavour. This approximates the advice handed down by Richard J. Doyle, who as editor-in-chief hired me for the editorial board at the Globe and Mail. *Beware the temptation to write purple prose, he said, or to toss in fancy words most readers would have to search for in a dictionary. You can allow yourself one plum in a piece of writing – people will forgive one, and make the effort to look it up or guess it from the context – but beyond that you try their patience and look like a show-off.*

Among my favourites in the challenge for the first drafts of song titles that cried out for adjustment:

"Ah, Sweet Mystery of Liver" JANE BRANT

"I'm Going to Sit Right Down and Write Myself a Résumé" FORBES HELEM

"Parsley, Sage, Rosemary and Ketchup" ALANNA LITTLE

"Mack the Fork" CHARLES CROCKFORD

"I Want to Hold Your Calls" JENNIFER D. HUGHES

"We Are the Developed Countries" BARBARA S. WANLESS

"How Much Is That Pit Bull in the Window" MARY ELLEN & PETER SALMON

Perhaps *to place myself in the shoes of that perplexed reader, I opened the gates a year later to entries about opera, a subject about which I have, to borrow the title of one of Oscar Levant's autobiographies,* A Smattering of Ignorance. *But then, that's why they publish*

reference books. A childhood spent examining the album covers of my father's record collection (much Wagner) helped.

The challenge was to amend a well-known opera to give it a more prosaic theme. The idea came from John Summers, whose example was Götterdämmer-ladder-rung: *A sad tale of a home handyman's misfortune. Other sterling rewrites:*

Der Frozenkavalier: Mounted soldier gets northern posting.

MIKE ENGLAND

Die Flattermaus: How a man with a steamroller built a better mousetrap. JENNIFER STRATTON

False Staff: A manager is arrested after making up fake personnel lists. GEOFF WILLIAMS

Un Ballo in Mascara: A Mary Kay representative gets disappointing results from an elaborate cosmetics sales party.

JEF TEN KORTENAAR

The Rinse Cycle: Mythological figures and ordinary Torontonians mingle in a Laundromat. HIRSH JACOBSON

La Triviata: A forgettable adaptation of Shakespeare's *Much Ado About Nothing*. FRANK HAIGH

Die Walkies: The Barbara Woodhouse story.

SIMON ELLIOTT PARKER

The Babar of Seville: Tale of the Spanish Elephant Man.

STELLA SCOTT

Lornegreen: The story of one of Canada's great voices.

CELINE PAPIZEWSKA

Babar of Seville

Die, Meistersinger, Die: A slasher opera with a low-rent
Phantom. PHILIP STREET

Fido and Aeneas: A man and his dog.
PHIL & TARA COLLINGTON

Ring of the Feeblelungen: The CBC's smokers circle passes the
butt around. ANITA NOEL & DAVID ANTSCHERL

Lab Ho-Hum: Life goes on at Parke-Davis. RUSSELL YAPP

Il Trouve a Tory: Bilingual opera of the amazing discovery
of a man in Quebec who voted for the Conservative
Party in the last election. GEOFF WILLIAMS

Low 'n' Grin: Bucolic story of contented cows.
NATALIA MAYER

The Yesman of the Guard: A young officer has a nose for
quick promotion. BARRIE COLLINS

UNTRUSTWORTHY ADVICE

The gist of this Challenge was simple. Imagine the worst advice or explanation you could give to a tourist or new immigrant: misleading, unreliable, certain to land the unfortunate soul in all sorts of trouble. Brendan J. O'Byrne suggested this one after reading a report from the Canadian Press of real-life "wacky questions fielded by Canadian tourist offices." Among them: Do your hotel rooms have mirrors on the ceiling? Is your civil war over yet (referring to the Quebec referendum)? How long would it take to swim to Victoria from Vancouver (a distance of eighty kilometres)?

Patrick Gage offered a few cod-historical facts – among them, "In Canadian politics, the Upper House is called the Sennett, after Mack Sennett of the Keystone Kops" – and added, "I wouldn't mind the job of creating a history text with 'facts' such as these. Beats the hell out of names and dates!" Linda Lumsden asked, "Are you sure you didn't get this idea from Monty Python?" – a reference, presumably, to the skit in which a hapless customer tries to communicate with a shopkeeper using a phrasebook with maliciously inaccurate translations.

Examples of untrustworthy advice:

Canadians always like to hear how to improve their country
by making it more like the U.S.A.

AURORA MENDELSOHN

Canadians are known as friendly, accommodating and
docile, so feel free to cut in at the front of supermarket
and theatre queues; it's expected.

Be sure to take along an adequate supply of raw meat and
honey to hand-feed the lovable grizzly bears in Canada's
national parks.

If a customs or immigration officer asks you a question you
consider too personal, don't be afraid to say, "I don't
think that's any of your business."   W.P. KINSELLA

When you see unoccupied chairs in a restaurant, feel free to
join strangers at their table. In Canada, it is considered
an honour if a foreigner eats off your plate.   ANN KNIGHT

Tourists who are not feeling well may obtain a free physical
examination from 1:00 a.m. to 3:00 a.m. on any street
corner in Toronto's Parkdale district.

Touch new acquaintances (especially women) on the arm
or shoulder.

Talk in an elevator.

Praise Canadian governments.   JONATHAN USHER

The Jamaican custom of strict punctuality requires that visitors should endeavour to be early for all appointments.
                                    T. & F. GUNN

Georgia state troopers believe in the principle that you are
innocent until proven guilty, and therefore welcome an
argument.   LINDA LUMSDEN

To eliminate bureaucracy and overhead, Canadian religions
practise random redistribution of wealth. If the person
next to you puts a donation in the collection plate, you
should take money out. Rule of thumb: bigger church,
bigger handful.   HUGH CAMPBELL

If you want a good table in a Las Vegas nightclub, don't bribe the maitre d'. It's first come, first served.

RUTH BROWN

The swingers scene in Saudi Arabia is legendary.

ALEXANDER J. BALDWIN

In Dublin, you are expected to return your first Guinness to the publican, complaining (in an Irish accent) that it lacks body.
During guided tours of the Plains of Abraham, it is customary to sing "Rule Britannia."

JIM PARR

Fun-loving airport personnel all over the world enjoy a good laugh, so have lots of drug and bomb jokes ready when you are having your luggage scanned.

HELEN MCCUSKER

To show respect in Mohawk territories, address any adult male you meet as "Chief."

SUSAN CAMPBELL

The Scots, Welsh and Irish all love to be called "English."

AL WILKINSON

Quebeckers love to practise their English on visitors, but
they tend to be shy, so, even if you speak French, insist
that they speak English.　　HELEN & PETER MARUCCI

The best restaurants in France always reserve a bottle of
ketchup for their more discriminating guests, so be
sure to ask.
The purpose of Question Period in the House of Commons
is to gain answers to questions.
Any RCMP officer will be only too glad to whistle you a few
bars of "Rose Marie."
Dehydration can be a problem in Mexico, so drink several
glasses of water (the cold tap is *F* for *frío*) each day.

KEN PURVIS

The Laurentian Shield is a Canadian contraceptive device.

STEPHEN NOTAR

"Yeah, right!" means the speaker completely believes in
everything you just said.　　GORDON FINDLAY

"Let's do lunch" means the person will call you for lunch.

ALANNA LITTLE

Taxis are best hailed with the middle finger raised,
"Trudeau-style."
During Question Period, the PM invites questions from the
visitors' gallery.
Tipping is an offence carrying severe penalties.

BRENDAN J. O'BYRNE

Canada is a land of heroes. Any Canadian will be proud to
recount the famous deeds of our citizens.　　K.C. ANGUS

163

COUPLETS

O ver the years, the Challenge has requested couplets on the topic of tax time, on holiday traffic, on the extinction of animals, on insects and in praise of ordinary things. After entering the animal-extinction contest, K.C. Angus wrote, "There. Now for a beef sandwich and then I'll send my annual donation to the SPCA."

A number of these entries are by Barrie Collins. In 1999, he was the subject of a double-page article by Marilyn Simms in InFocus Magazine, published in Mr. Collins's home town of Courtenay, B.C. The title: "Completely Challenged." "Collins wins The Challenge about once a year," she wrote, "but his witticisms receive honourable mention almost weekly – 'Often quite weakly,' he says with a laugh – with a personal record of eleven consecutive weeks."

As the fellow at the receiving end of his lovely work, I was intrigued to read of Mr. Collins's routine. "His inventive mind is active from the Saturday morning when he first reads The Challenge to the following weekend when, after many revisions, he faxes his entry to that putative centre of Canada, Toronto." As with other contributors whose biographical details have come my way, he has a history of this sort of thing, having written songs and skits for Christmas parties at Teleglobe Canada Inc., where he worked for three decades, and having put out a satirical newspaper.

There are times when I regret my monkish insistence on not

meeting with members of the Challengentsia for fear of compromis-
ing (or being seen to compromise) my objectivity in the judging. Mr.
Collins mentioned in the article that he had been invited (but had
declined) to fly to Toronto for a gathering of ten or so Challengers.
Stewart Fisher, in a postscript to one of his entries, wrote: "You might
be interested to know that because of the Challenge, Alanna Little
and I are having lunch in the Executive dining room of the Canadian
Imperial Bank of Commerce on March 13, 1998. We have not met
before." It's a bit like knowing a party is going on that you can't
attend because of a prior commitment, though it's safe to say the real
party takes place on the page each week.

At another point, Helen McCusker wrote of having met another
Challenge contributor, Ken Purvis, and engaging in "an animated
and interesting (to us) conversation and discussion on strategies for
getting our entries published: Should one wait until the last minute
and fax them so they're fresh in the memory at deadline time, or send
them in as soon as possible, so they are chosen before the editors over-
dose? Also, is it better to go for quantity, overwhelming you with sheer
volume, or just send in the best of the crop (thereby sparing you some-
what)?" To the first question, I read them all in one sitting. To the
second, yes, edit for quality, thank you. I read them all in one sitting.

I have here the chance to make it up to Helen Poole for an odd
inadvertence in the publication of a 1993 compilation of Challenge
entries. The book carried her poem on the back cover, duly credited,
but it somehow was omitted inside the covers. Here it is, along with
a host of other choice couplets written over the years:

An ant is not a household pet.
He does not seem to know that yet.   HELEN POOLE

Without the humble kitchen chair
We'd all be sitting in mid-air.   EDWARD BAXTER

Said Marquis de Sade at a job interview,
I prefer tax collector, but hangman'll do.

Though death and taxes are both bores
Death at least won't do encores.   ZENON YARYMOWICH

The last great ape said not to grieve.
"I remain in the gene pool of Adam and Eve."

The woolly mammoth, warm-clad beast,
Attracted moths, and so deceased.

The hippopotamus, bored with wallowing,
Took up jogging, extinction following.   KEN PURVIS

The leopard, told it couldn't change its spots,
Gave way to suicidal thoughts.   B.W. JACKSON

Is the sudden death of lepidoptera
Caused by the blades of helicoptera?

If thoroughbreds die out before us,
We'll sing the Hialeah Chorus.   BARRIE COLLINS

The praying mantis eats its hubby.
Serial monogamy would make it chubby.
                         NANCY MITCHELL

Language is graphic
In holiday traffic.   K.C. ANGUS

He thought the carphone was a great invention.
St. Peter's now asking for his extension.
                         CHARLES CROCKFORD

Let's mourn the passing of the turtle.
He lost the knack of being fertile.   BARRIE COLLINS

The threatened hippopotamus
Doesn't think a lot of us.   WILLIAM G. ALEXANDER

The cockroach thrives while panda bears lose ground.
What a shame it's not the other way around.
                                        ARTHUR M. LIPMAN

The dinosaur lay down to die.
"At least I know they'll wonder why."   ALANNA MATTHEW

The elephant expired in a funk.
The airline had misplaced his trunk.   P. HUTCHINGS

"When I'm gone, the garden'll
Be lifeless," said the cardinal.

Relentless was the mantis-slaying.
Ironic, after all that praying.   JIM PARR

The passenger pigeon was fun to shoot.
If you look for it now you will find it kaput.
                                        HELEN J. HUGET

Many animals at the zoo
Die of boredom. Wouldn't you?   FRANK HAIGH

Our cat, who'd had nine lives, tried for ten.
Amen.   EARL A. OLMSTED

A cruel joke
If all frogs croak.   STEWART FISHER

Why are some fierce and others placid?
Deoxyribonucleic acid!   BRIAN RYAN

Too bad the great auk
Didn't know how to talk.   L.E. JONES

The fruit fly's life is very, very
Short twixt birth and cemetery.   GEORGE F. ROGERS

An epitaph: Beneath this stone
I lie. I lie! 'Tis but my clone.   JIM PARR

There twice was a man from Nantucket.
He was cloned in a lab, in a bucket.   JEFF MCCARTNEY

When Dolly i became Dolly ii,
Was it a case of déjà ewe?   GEOFF WILLIAMS

Downsize this office, the consultant said.
Now the consultant does my work instead.

CRAIG CHERRIE

In executive hiring, one rule is immutable:
Whoever the president fancies is suitable.

GORDON FINDLAY

The technophobe and the technophile are less different
    than once thought.
The phobe has crashed a hard drive, while the phile to date
    has not. RON CHARACH

He sat there at his desk and wept
Because his space had not been swept. K.M. JOHNSTON

When staff begin to grow too wise
Smart managers reorganize. JIM PARR

In times of change, be resilient.
Tell your boss his idea's brilliant. BARRIE COLLINS

tell your boss his idea's brilliant

After the season's eggnog and grog,
No man's agog at his own physiog. JOSEPH E. DONNELLY

I'll jog, eat less and lose this fat.
(But hey, if you're not going to finish that . . .) J.I. CATES

The mynah mocked the sparrow's pleas
Who promptly sued for royalties.   DON RYAN

The Hereford steer's naive belief
Is that we humans don't like beef.   BARRIE COLLINS

A mousetrap is a great device
Not highly thought of by the mice.   HELEN PERRY

Because he leaves a trail of slime,
The slug eschews a life of crime.   ALANNA MATTHEW

A kitchen clean beyond reproach
Can nonetheless sustain the roach.   KEN PURVIS

It's hard for a kid to stay mentally focused
When he's writing a report on *The Day of the Locust*.

PETER WARREN

Fire ants do not have a hall.
Engines? Hoses? None at all.   C.H. VANE-HUNT

The cicada calls for lovers way up in the tree:
"I'm here! I'm here! Oh, please pick me!"   PHIL PYE

Trap door spiders are remarkably clever.
Their victims remain surprised forever.   JEANNE DENEE

Why God created wasps I fail to see.
No doubt they feel the same regarding me.

JACK HARRYMAN

I don't understand how some creatures are rated.
A goldfish is loved but a silverfish hated.   KARL DILCHER

Everybody wants to be that "fly on the wall,"
But nobody wants to hear the swatter fall. PAUL KOCAK

When Shall We Three Meet Again?

The three wise men, the three witches, three on a match, the third man – you can't go wrong with three, unless you'd been counting on a good game of bridge.

Over the years the Challenge has set several contests predicated on the number three. One of them was to compose a sequence of nouns with a descending level of respect, depending on whether the nouns referred to me, you or them. For instance: *My truth, your opinion, his prejudices (George Kraemer). My nectar of the gods, your wine, his plonk (Edward Baxter). My abs, your middle, his gut (Bryan Cummings).*

Another was on the baroque side: *Create inappropriate trios and supply rhyming explanations for them. A deer, a melon and a shy southern belle: an antelope, a cantaloupe and "ah shan't elope" (Jim Parr); John Wayne, Danny Kaye and "The White Cliffs of Dover": gritty, Mitty, ditty (Helen and Trevor Giles); Casper, Curaçao and Cromwell: spectre, nectar and Protector (Dick and Sue Waterman).* The Watermans wrote: "We found this to be a deceptively difficult one. We threw out several pages of offerings that came quickly to the mind but which were utterly stupid, leaving just these few. Hopefully Mr. B. Collins and some of the other regulars can come up with something more worthy." *Barrie Collins did indeed make an appearance,* with *New Mexico place, pemmican base, the whole human race: Albuquerque, jerky, quirky.*

A third assignment, and the most popular of the bunch if the number of entries is anything to by, was this: Compose a phrase with three words – the first a real name, and the second a bridge between the first and third (as in Pol Pot pie) – and define the result. This they did:

Fletcher Christian Dior: Designer label for the well-dressed mutineer.

D'Oyly Carte blanche: Full permission to perform Gilbert and Sullivan.

Robert Frost bite: What you get for stopping by woods on a snowy evening.

Céline Dion Quintuplets: Five-girl singing group.

John Deere John: Letter in which a farm wife explains to her husband that she has wrecked the tractor. FRED FARR

Richard Gere shift: Conversion to another religion.

GLEN ACORN

Moby Dick Tracy: A sailor is obsessed with solving the mystery of the disappearing whales. BERT GASKELL

moby dick tracy

Alice Munro Doctrine: The idea that Canadian literature
has a manifest destiny to sweep all of North America.

PAUL DAVY

Pierre Elliott Gould: A performer with a Streisand complex.

DAN RAFFERTY

Rodney King Kong: A guy the Los Angeles cops should
never, ever mess with.   HELEN & PETER MARUCCI

John Milton Bradley: Creator of the board game Pair of
Dice Lost.   STEPHEN DUDZIK

Robin Hood ornament: Souvenir from your visit to
Sherwood Forest.

JOHN ILLINGWORTH & NORMA CRAWFORD

James Bond trader: Licensed to fill orders.   COLIN EYSSEN

Karl Marx Brothers: Starring Pinko.   M. CHRISTOPHER

Courtney Love handles: Middle-aged grunge.

JAMIE THOMPSON

Alexander Mackenzie King: Explorer who sought the
Northwest Passage if necessary, but not necessarily
the Northwest Passage.   GORD TOLTON

Kim Campbell Soup: Soup with an unpopular flavour,
withdrawn after a few months.   VAL & JAMES DUTHIE

Julia Child bride: A young girl who is married off early
because she is a good cook.   MALKIN HOWES

Immanuel Kant Wynn: A philosopher of the German
Pessimist school.   PAUL DAVY

Ludwig Van Lines: Carefully orchestrated removals.

JIM PARR

Ivan the Terrible Headache: Not tonight, Czarina.

KATHI WILLIAMS

Arthur Conan Barbarian: Hollywood hack who rewrites complex mysteries as mindless shootouts. AL WILKINSON

Joyce Brothers Grimm: The psychological side of fairy tales.

LINDA LUMSDEN

Lloyd Robertson screwdriver: A device to anchor news to the wall. MARK TRUEMAN

Emily Post Haste: A condensed course of modern etiquette.

JUDITH NEALE

Della Street Walker: Perry Mason's Friday-night gal.

HELEN PERRY

TALES OF THE FANTASTIC

When *Jules Verne wrote* From the Earth to the Moon *more than a century ago, moon travel was no more than a fond fantasy. Suppose one were writing a book today that would appear similarly unrealistic or fantastic to a reader in the early twenty-first century. What would the title be?*

When I set this contest in 1999, I was grappling with my own futuristic dilemma. Should the Challenge accept entries by e-mail? Readers had been pressing for this easy way to submit their material, and I had been hemming and hawing. The problem was not that I felt uncomfortable around technology. If the squirrels inside the computer monitor could run in place fast enough to keep electricity flowing to my screen, I was prepared to advance along with everyone else. No, I was just worried about the greater volume of mail and the additional time it would take to give that mail the attention it deserved.

On June 3, 2000, I bit the bullet and included the e-mail address. It took a few weeks to persuade the computer not to break and hyphenate it after the second e in challenge, but that was the only hurdle. As expected, the number of entries rose, and, as hoped, the quality remained high; people weren't just dashing them off. The occasionally tiresome task of transferring all the electronic entries to my text system was offset by the fact that I didn't have to type them *in. I still prefer paper, but then I'm also fond of vinyl* LPS *and manually operated can openers.*

I digress. Here is a list of titles that might seem as unrealistic or fantastic today as From the Earth to the Moon *did in the nineteenth century.*

The Comedian Who Never Swore.
The Undisturbed Loner.
Not Enough Lawyers.
The Blockbuster Movie With Absolutely No Fast-Food Tie-Ins,
    Toys or Merchandising of Any Kind.   MEG SULLIVAN

The Handwritten Letter.   PATRICIA TRIPP

the handwritten letter

We So Loved the Government.   GORDON FINDLAY

Twenty Thousand Dollars Under the Estimate.
The Guy Who Said He'd Call – and Did!   SANDRA HULL

The Airport Baggage Carousel That Did Not Make a
    Screeching Noise As If It Were in Severe Pain.
                                    JOHN O'BYRNE

The Adolescent Who Hated Phones.
The Edible Store-Bought Tomato.   T.W. MORLEY

The Royal Couple Who Lived Happily Ever After.
Memoirs of a CEO: I Failed and Have No One to Blame But
    Myself.   ALANNA LITTLE

My MP Visited Between Elections.   JIM PARR

Drink Deep of Thee, Mother Ganges.
                                        DICK & SUE WATERMAN

The Student Who Came to School Without a Cell, Pager or
    Lawyer.   BRIAN PASTOOR

The Man Who Stopped at a Red Light.   BILL STRIDER

Middle East Peace for Dummies.   MARCELLO GROSSUTTI

BORN UNDER A BAD SPELLING

Few things in life offer as much entertainment value as the common typographical error. Journalists live in fear of spelling public as pubic – perhaps not the same degree of fear as reporters on the front lines of Afghanistan, but fear nonetheless. So readers were asked to compose a newspaper headline containing a significant typographical error.

I resisted the impulse to explain entries that erred on the obscure side. Trust the reader. If a laugh follows, great. If a belly laugh follows, somewhere an angel will get his wings.

Ronald Ferrie submitted a couple of headlines – "Two Large ww2 Boobs Found in London Excavation," and "Cleric Observed Kissing in Pubic" – to which he appended the line "With a credit to Lawrence Durrell." Durrell fans may be surer of what he means than I am.

Ian Brown could "not resist plagiarizing and updating a British classic: 'Gen. Norman Schwarzkopf: Gulf War Battle-Scared Veteran.' Which would be restated with an apology the following day as: 'Gen. Norman Schwarzkopf: Gulf War Bottle-Scarred Veteran.'"

Andy Séguin sent a fax from Singapore with this one: "United Nations Pronounces Erections Free and Fair." I'm not sure how he saw the Globe and Mail there, this being in 1996, well before the newspaper put all its contents on-line. Which probably explains his request. "If published, could we get a copy of the subject G&M sent to us. It's not easy to get here in Singapore, thanks."

Chris Hurst, in offering this one about Canada's former prime minister – *Mulroney Indicted into Canadian Hall of Fame* – prefaced it with this note: "I feel badly picking on Brian, but no one else I tried sounded as funny in the joke."

Paul Davy included a noteworthy "headline I really saw in the Globe *last year: a front-page item listing the articles which were* '*Notworthy Inside.*' "

Peter Marucci, at one time a Toronto journalist, prefaced his list of entries with this line: "Hi there. Doing the 'headline' Challenge was just like being back at the Star *– except there are fewer typos in today's offerings.*"

The Challenge is not about to cast the first stone. Over the years, I have made a few embarrassing mistakes. Sometimes they were errors of commission, one of which drew this letter from David Dunsmuir. "*I suggested* My Favourite La Manchan *as a title for a* TV *sitcom about Don Quixote; you printed this with no final 'n.' I now find that both versions, as submitted and (presumably) as edited, were inaccurate. After tracking this down in Don Quixote itself, I find that the locative form is Manchegan, with no article.*" For my part, I lopped off the "n" accidentally.

When John Morrissey won a Challenge, he wrote to say he looked forward to receiving the prize book, but was less delighted that I had placed him in Ottawa instead of Owen Sound. John O'Byrne lives in Dublin and his brother Brendan O'Byrne in Regina. When I inadvertently placed Brendan in Dublin, he sent in copies of other contests (*Mary Ann Madden's wonderful long-running one in* New York *magazine, and the column "Bob Levey's Washington" in the* Washington Post*) in which both he and his brother were mentioned. He wrote:* "Both the Washington Post *and* NY Mag. Comp. *cannot be wrong!*"

Sometimes they are errors of omission, ones I should have caught but didn't. A Challenge about suitable businesses for historical or literary characters drew the entry "Herod's the Hand Towel People." Alas, it was Pontius Pilate, not Herod, who infamously washed his hands.

Sometimes they are errors of haste. In response to a Challenge about logical occupations based on celebrities' names, B.W. Jackson submitted (along with "Clark Gable: roofer," and "Saul Bellow: town *crier") the answer "Alexandr Pushkin: geneoligist." I was transcribing it quickly, realized there was a spelling mistake, but for some reason corrected it as gynecologist. Mr. Jackson responded: "I thought 'genealogist' (even spelled wrongly) was not bad for Pushkin, but I like 'gynecologist' too, even though I can take no credit for it."*

The question of taste surfaces every week, since a few readers invariably turn off their inner censors while responding to the assignment. The line between what can run in a daily newspaper and what can't is fairly clear, and entrants acknowledge the fact. Glen Acorn, after submitting this erroneously altered headline – Pollsters Detect Shit in Voter Attitudes – attached a postscript: "I know you can't print this one but I threw it in anyway."

Similarly, though the language was milder, Mike Snipper provided an option when he submitted this quatrain: "Strange though it may sound, the porcupine/ Is neither tree nor swine./ One must assume the naming naturalist/ Was pissed." He offered this alternative ending: "Reasons for the blunder are never stated./ One assumes the nominator was inebriated."

Barrie Collins, entering the Challenge on comments you wouldn't expect to hear from professionals, ended his letter with this line: "And then, of course, there's the proctologist's lament that he'd only failed his gynecology exam by that *much. But this is a family newspaper, after all."*

Beyond the four-letter words, I am squeamish on behalf of the many thousands of readers eating their breakfast on a Saturday morning. So bodily fluids are generally right out; in fact, it is their being right out that triggers the taste alarm.

Here are the best of the typographically challenged headlines that did make the cute – sorry, cut:

Atlantic Fishermen Warned God Will Not Return for
Generations.   JACK ORBAUM

Choir Director Latest Victim of Rising Alto Thefts.
                                                DAVID STUBBS

Bosnian Verbs Cause Difficulties.   TONY CHANDLER

Hostages Breed After Long Ordeal.   MICHAEL BREND

PM Starts Cabinet Scuffle.   KARL DILCHER

Prince Charles Says He Will Never Give Up the Clown.

BRENDA M. CORR

Palace Rumour: Fergie's Royal Bonking Privileges
  Withdrawn.   JIM PARR

Charles Claims Di Betrayed His Tryst.   CHRIS HURST

Figures Support New Brunswick's Job Cremation Policy.

BRUCE C.W. MCFARLANE

FIB Agent Sentenced for Perjury. L.J. KOH

Premier Seeks Support for Daft Legislation. GLEN ACORN

Unemployed Miners Burrowing to Pay Debts.
BRIAN EVANS

Baker Saves Local Boy from Browning. TREVOR GILES

The Bird is the Word

Challenge headquarters is an abstract concept. Readers know I'm the compère of the operation, but beyond that all is murky. I receive letters that salute me as "Dear people" or that begin: "Would you or somebody on your staff be able to send me a column from two years ago that had something to do with oranges?"

There is no staff. There is me. No, I lie; Suzanne Buhasz, whose organizational skills keep several sections of the Globe and Mail from spinning off into space, kindly mails off the prizes when I remember to give her the appropriate lists. But other than that, it's a bare-bones operation, or as bare as bones can be when fed a regular diet of Globe and Mail cafeteria food.

The Challenge compère works at a desk in a cubicle surrounded by colleagues who are quietly industrious or demonstrably noisy, but all delightful people, none of whom owes me money. In the early days, my cubicle was on the second floor of the Globe's building. The desk subsequently moved to the third floor, and then back down to the second floor. This is what passes for exercise in my life.

For the first few years, after the Facts and Arguments editor in the next cubicle had gone home for the day, the spot was filled by Peter Whelan. Peter, who died too young, was a phenomenon. His day job had something to do with making millions on the stock market – whether for himself or others I was never quite sure – but once a week *he would write the* Globe and Mail*'s widely read bird column. (That is, the column was widely read. I can't speak for the birds.) He would sit down at the telephone and methodically call his contacts in cities and towns from Newfoundland to British Columbia – in that order, because Newfoundlanders would be going to bed about the time British Columbians would be getting home from work. He would start phoning people on the East Coast to find out who had seen which birds during the week, and move west through the time zones.*

My wife-to-be, Sandra, turned out to be an avid birder and a great fan of Peter Whelan. She also liked "Nestlings," a comic strip I drew for the Globe. *Since the subject was birds, she naturally assumed I would know a lot about them. I knew nothing about them, apart from a trip to the encyclopedia to make sure robins ate worms. I know more now, but only because the obvious points stick in the mind: Cardinals are red, blue jays are blue, starlings are a nuisance and chances are the bird you're looking at, however intriguing, is a sparrow.*

With this experience, it was only natural that the Challenge would set a bird contest. One of them, to record the calls of little-known birds, drew responses mainly about current politics (although Procter Le Mare offered the Suburban Car-Alarm Turkey: Wee oo wee oo wee oo):

Paykist's Grouse: See-ceed. See-ceed.   DON SUTHERS

The Question Period turkey: Gobble, gobbledygook.
ALANNA LITTLE

The Lesser Thatcher Bird: Too-wet-to-win, too-wet-to-win.
ALASTAIR URQUHART

The Western Breast-Beating Senate Bird: E-E-E.
STUART ALCOCK

The *other ornithological challenge was to alter the name of a bird and suggest a corresponding change in habitat, diet, song or behaviour.*

Ken Purvis wrote to say he had spent a happy morning in the reference library poring over Birds of the World: A Checklist, *by James*

F. Clements, designed by his wife Christina Clements. "Any connection?" Not that I know of. "He lists nine thousand birds! I hope you don't have to weed through close to that number from avid birder-contestants. There are 215 species of tanagers alone (including a lacrimose tanager – unfortunately, probably too obscure for a Challenge entry). You'll get many 'teenager' ideas, such as 'Scarlet Teenager: Congregating in noisy high-spirited groups, exhibiting variant head colours but otherwise with a certain conformity of plumage.'"

Jack Barnes offered four written pages of entries, prefaced with an apology for the profusion, "but I must admit I just got carried away with the novel idea of your Challenge, and I like birds! The following are the ramblings of an eighty-year-old mind that doesn't recognize moderation in an age of excess." They weren't rambling, and among them was the Canadian Silverfinch: tries to compete with its American cousin, the goldfinch, but usually comes in second.

A few other species from a packed aviary:

Cedar Faxwing: Highly evolved bird that employs tele-communications instead of bird song.   LINDA ROBB

Stuffed Grouse: Elusive oven-ready game bird.

ROBIN LOVELL

Pleated Woodpecker: Has uniquely folded feathers.

ANNE RONEY

Vowl: Night hunter identified by its call of "AEIOU."
Purple Martian: Bird with the longest migration route.

AL WILKINSON

Evening Grosspeak: Nocturnal bird indigenous to city parks. Song is a series of loud, strident noises accompanied by rude language.
Chickapea: Small European migrant; feeds mainly on garbanzo beans.

SANDRA L. JONES & CATHY FURGIUELE

Purple Flinch: A nervous and twitchy bird, easily startled.

CHRISTINE DUGDALE

Hooded Mergangster: Duck that terrorizes other birds and steals their eggs.

Glossy Ibid: Long-legged wader, always seen in the same place.

GEOFFREY PIERPOINT

Baltimore Oreo: Eats the middle of his food first.

LINDA LUMSDEN

Toucam: Has miniature camera in its bill for live Webcasts.

PAUL KOCAK

Thumbingbird: Has learned to alleviate the stress of lengthy migrations by hitchhiking.   C.H. VANE-HUNT

Long-Billed Curfew: A quiet bird, rarely seen after nightfall.

JAY BOOKER

thumbingbird

Hamming Pigeon: Will imitate William Shatner for food.

G. TREFLAK

Wordpicker: A pedantic parrot.   TONY CHANDLER

Whopping Crane: The gargantuan appetite of this colossal
creature has put it on the endangered list.   KEN PURVIS

Erring Gull: With the unusual trait of heading north in the
fall and south in the spring.   F.H. BELLSTEDT

Robin Bedrest: Lesser red-feathered bird of the malingerer
family.   MIKE R. HARRIS

Tatmouse: Often offered in return for the titmouse.

MEG SULLIVAN

Cuckolds: Birds that mate for life with partners that don't.

ELIZABETH & CHARLES BIGELOW

TWO'S A CROWD

You have bought your ticket, settled into your airplane seat, pulled out that book you've been wanting to read and – fatal error – glanced at the person next to you. You are then treated to seven hours of earnest conversation about the cute things his or her children said that day, or the mechanical failures of other airplanes, or why it is so vitally important that one's loved ones be protected in the event of illness or death, and isn't it lucky your seatmate has a blank insurance form in his briefcase.

Keen to be of service as well as amusement, the Challenge asked readers to suggest ways to discourage unwanted conversation on a plane, bus or train.

Linda Francey offered a real-life conversation-stopper. "Midnight. I'm waiting for a bus in Windsor, when a rumpled man around forty sits beside me on the bench after asking if that's okay. I answer, sure, and we start chatting about the bus times, weather etc. After a quiet period, he says, 'They think I killed my mother.'"

"Below you will find," wrote William Gulycz, "my diplomatic (?) ways out of what sometimes promise to become long and tedious close encounters. I suppose the nature of your staff's work flings you all over the globe, including danger spots" – and he noted as a wry example that William Thorsell, then editor-in-chief of the Globe and Mail, had "braved the perils" of a conference in Davos, Switzerland.

"I therefore think it might be a humane service that after you've made your selections (publishable and unpublishable), you share them with the staff."

Nah, let's share them with everyone. Among the best lines to discourage unwanted conversation on a plane, bus or train:

"In the event some of my multiple personalities take over, my real name is Jim."

"My fellow actuaries tell me that with a little practice I could be a stand-up comic."

"Once we're under way, remind me to relate the fascinating history of the accelerated capital-cost-allowance provisions."

DWAYNE W. ROWE

"Do you believe in the afterlife? Let me tell you how I met the Supreme Being and what this has meant to me."

IAN BROWN

"Would you believe it? My Uzi didn't even set off the metal detector."

"do you believe in the afterlife?"

"It sure is nice of the Sex Offenders Clinic to fly me home on a weekend pass. Say, did anyone ever tell you that you have a beautiful smile?"

"Excuse me, ma'am, would you mind not talking so I can concentrate on putting this pin back in the grenade?"

IAN KAVANAGH

"I'm with Revenue Canada. What do you do?"

HEATHER MOWAT

"I always find it easier to discuss my personal problems with strangers."

"Would you care to hear the jokes I'm submitting to *Reader's Digest*?"

DIANE BETHUNE

"You know, *contagious* is only a word until you have something."

"Charlie Manson was a victim of bad press."

WILLIAM GULYCZ

"I like to sit at the back of the bus, so the driver can't see what I'm up to."

LINDA LUMSDEN

"Oh, I sell life insurance. Tough business. Do you have a family?"

"My problem is a hair-trigger temper. Sometimes the most innocent remark can set me off."

LEONARD WISE

"You know, I've had interesting dreams since I was a child. And I remember them all very clearly. The first one was about . . ."

EVA HECHT

"When we get to Customs, would you mind carrying my suitcase?"

ALANNA LITTLE

"May I have your paper bag? I find that one is not enough when I fly." STEWART FISHER

"Excuse me, it's silent prayer time for our cult leader. Will you join me?" ARTHUR GOOCH

"I should mention that I perspire a lot. But it's just the body cleansing itself. I find it much more natural than a bath." DAVID SAVAGE

"Yes, that's a lovely picture of your family. It reminds me of my own family before the train wreck." AL WILKINSON

"I used to be a maintenance worker on these things, and I can tell you some real horror stories."
"Do you ever imagine that your hands are growing into claws?" HELEN & PETER MARUCCI

"What do you think should be done about Canada's Constitution?" NANCY GOLDRING

"The waste in government is terrible. It's not fair that our guards should travel first-class while we prisoners have to sit in economy." ERIC MENDELSOHN

This contest was a close cousin of a column that ran the same year about startling things to say on an elevator. "As I live on the twenty-seventh floor," wrote Chris Hurst, "I spend a fair amount of time in elevators. So far, I have yet to be stuck in one, but these entries will probably anger the spirit/deity who is in charge of these things." Among the submissions: "The day before our engagement party isn't a good time to tell me you've had a sex-change operation" (Linda Lumsden). "I can prove my point by simultaneously pushing these three buttons. Ready?" (Jim Parr). "Did you say your flatulence increases with altitude?" (Ian Brown).

CHALLENGES-IN-WAITING

Some weeks the Challenge feels like a perpetual-motion machine. Not only do readers write the column (Ron Charach, who suggested I some day take a few of "the Globe Challenge'd" to lunch so they could meet each other, added: "Churning out all this free copy leaves one ravenous") but they supply most of the Challenges. The suggestions began soon after the column started, and grew exponentially as other readers realized the way was open. I happily harnessed their inspiration and use the ideas offered whenever they surpass my own, which is most of the time.

Inevitably, the pile of unused Challenges has grown. Sometimes I don't use a good idea because I can't see more than a couple of possible (at least, humorously possible) answers coming out of it. Sometimes the challenge has been used before, which is a shame when the examples provided are terrific. Sometimes the idea is so complicated that explaining the darned thing would take up half the column. Sometimes answering it would require specialized knowledge – fun for the handful of entrants who knew the subject inside-out, but less fun for the other Challengers and for readers.

The upshot is that my files are full of unused Challenges, many of them good enough to be offered on their own, as Challenges-in-waiting or amusing one-offs. Here are a few of them. The words are verbatim from the readers:

"Devise an opening sentence for the most politically incorrect book you can imagine. E.g.: 'From her first moment of consciousness, Millie just knew she couldn't wait to find a man who would care for her, buy her a large house and fill it with adorable babies.'" (George E. Jackson)

"Invent unsung heroes in the more mundane areas of life. For instance, whatever became of Minny Minny Moore, who used to have bottom billing on every K-Tel record?" (Barrie Collins)

"Come up with a book title, fiction or non-fiction, that is not likely to become a bestseller. Examples: *The Misunderstood Mosquito. Redundant Folds of Skin. Neurosurgery for Dummies.*" (Ron Charach)

"Have you ever thought of doing a Challenge based on poor typography in a newspaper headline? A couple of real-life examples: When the son of a mayor in a northern city came back home to set up his practice as a physiotherapist, the headline accidentally added a space: 'Mayor's Son Is The rapist.' Or perhaps we could come up with an interesting correction which appears in a newspaper. Another real-life example (I'm paraphrasing here) appeared in the Timmins *Daily Press*: We apologize for the error which appeared in a headline about the Mormon gathering in Kapuskasing on the first three thousand papers which were printed yesterday, in which the second *M* was dropped. To paraphrase Pogo: 'We have seen the moron, and it is us.'" (John K. Wroe)

"I would suggest favourable corporate mergers, such as Microsoft taking over the company that makes Viagra, or Nesbitt Burns merging with Pricewaterhouse." (Terry Killon)

There is one Challenge I would have loved to set, but it was *effectively commandeered by Roger Ebert, who compiled an entire book of examples with his readers' help and left little room for newcomers. The theme: Lessons I learned from the movies. Gary Borders of Cox News Service offered a few of them in a 1999 column, including* *these two: "During any police investigation, it will be necessary to visit a strip club at least once"; "When alone, foreigners prefer to speak English to each other."*

"According to a statement in Bill Casselman's book *Canadian Sayings* that was reported in the Social Studies column of July 21, there are 135 folk expressions that describe stupidity. Let's add to the list. E.g. His toilet is a gallon short of a flush. His garden is planted, but the seeds aren't up." (Charles Crockford)

"What are some of the signs to watch for an economic downturn? Example: Bank branches begin closing, leaving behind farewell messages written in soap on their windows. Diners in restaurants ask to pay for the meal before it comes, while the currency is still holding." (Ron Charach)

"Write a musical allusion of nine words, the initial letters of which follow a diatonic scale. E.g. (C major) Conductors Don't Ever Forgive Garbling a Bach Choral." (Jim Parr)

"Who drives what and what are the vanity plates? E.g. Bach drives a (Honda) Prelude with licence plate FUGUE. An Australian drives an Outback with licence plate GDAYM8." (Dave and Diane Hieatt)

"Suggest film epics on the extinction of the dinosaurs. *Apocalypse Then. The Big Chill. Jurassic Parka.*" (The Keogh family)

"Pet peeves of superheroes. E.g. Batman: Hates it when the change falls out of his pockets while sleeping upside-down. Catwoman: Fleas. Superman (Man of Steel): Rust. Spider-Man: Raid." (Doug Lalonde and Tim Keogh)

One contest was to suggest unfortunately named investments. *Financial analyst Chris Evans suggested a challenge based on the mangled language found in "Internet chat rooms, sometimes called forums. I've encountered many malapropisms, many of an unintended* *anatomical nature. For example: 'This is a takeover target. Over fifty investors want to get at their family jewels.' Or: 'This airline's crack-up value is . . .' I could go on."* Mr. Evans added: *"Like you, I am under constant pressure to publish, in my case several times monthly. I have read your column with interest and envy you. What other writer has the luxury of relying on his readers for not only the bulk of his current column but the topic of the next? Grrrrr."*

What can I say? I'm a lucky guy.

"Canadians are turning to natural medicines and treatments as never before. Slightly alter the title of a famous book, poem, play or movie to cater to the popular rise of acupuncture, herbal medicines, homeopathy et cetera. E.g., *Anthony and Chiropractor, Ginsengin' in the Rain.*" (Brian Pastoor)

"Medical conditions and their lesser-known causes. E.g., Cauliflower ear: A condition in young people attributed to fatigue following a parental admonition, 'You're not going anywhere until you finish your vegetables!'" (Chris Gosling).

"It's only natural at mid-career to consider a change in occupations. Cite some of the more karmic choices. Examples: An airline pilot tries her wings as a runway model. A coal miner decides to take up hard rock. An obstetrician opens a little takeout and delivery." (Ron Charach)

"Haste encourages us to use abbreviations. Therefore, we don't have time to check for inconsistencies or double meanings in their application. Illustrated with examples in question form. E.g. Vancouver clocks may be a few hours behind those in Toronto, but isn't 'Vancouver, B.C.' an insulting exaggeration?" (Al Wilkinson)

Alex *Macleod suggested the following marvellous idea, which struck me as entirely too much work. I have no doubt entrants would have been scrupulous in using only real lines from real poems, but it* *would have been hard for me to double-check, which is something editors like to do to earn what they fondly imagine to be a living wage.*

"In this week's Books section, Lynn Crosbie composed a poem from a pastiche of lines from different poets in the new Griffin anthology. I propose a Challenge to compose a quatrain consisting of the first lines of four different poems by different authors, or the first two lines of two poems by different authors. Here is an example of each (and their authors):

Turning and turning in the widening gyre
I caught this morning morning's minion,
Some say the world will end in fire,
And death shall have no dominion.
(Yeats, Hopkins, Frost, Thomas)

Call the roller of big cigars,
The muscular one, and bid him whip
Anyone lived in a pretty how town
(with up so floating many bells down)
(Stevens, cummings)."

S *tanley Walker suggested asking for highly unlikely names for restaurants, and suggested as examples the Heimlich Diner, the Fat Vat and the Rat's Whisker. Entertaining as those were, I could imagine hundreds more in the same vein arriving at my desk, and wasn't sure I was willing to interrupt readers' breakfasts in this fashion. Mr. Walker had the same idea for pubs: The Bloated Belly, The Demerit Point Inn, The Lost Weekend. And for nightclubs: The Blocked Fire Exit, Sweat City.*

"Suggest song titles incorporating food. E.g., 'Twinkie, Twinkie.' Or: 'How Are Things in Guacamole.' Or: 'Mousse Indigo.'" (Irma Coucill)

"Devise a book title that seems very appropriate or completely inappropriate to a particular publisher. Examples: *Ventriloquism for Dummies*. *Musical Boat Rides*, published by Harper & Row. *How to Organize Your Home*, published by Random House." (R.M. Liptrap)

The following mental twister came in a cross-office note from my colleague Sandy McFarlane.

"How many prepositions can you end a sentence with? Who are we aiming this Challenge on how many prepositions you can end a sentence with at? And who are we addressing this question about who we are aiming this challenge on how many prepositions you can end a sentence with at to?"

"Describe something Canadian as if it were a pasta dish. Examples:
Cape Breton – This rustic plate consists of a hearty oat-based pasta boiled in salt water. It is tossed with cabers and served with tartani sauce on a bed of dulse and garnished with a sugar-dipped bay leaf called Glace Bay." (Eric Mendelsohn)

"When the Mayor of Carlisle, who was about to demit office next day, discovered that he had impounded the horse of Robert Burns, he gave orders for it to be released, exclaiming, 'Let him have it by all means or the circumstance will be heard of for ages to come.' Burns took him up on this and penned the following quatrain:

Was e'er puir Poet sae befitted,
The maister drunk – the horse committed.
Puir harmless beast, tak thee nae care,
Thou'lt be a horse when he's nae mair.

Just as 'mair' sounds like, and can mean, mayor, mare and more, devise a triple pun using this form." (W.C. Watson)

"Ironic opposites. Would you shop at Unsafeway? Would Hitler have been able to defeat the Brits under Loseton Churchill? Would you like to live in Poormond Hill, north of Toronto?" (John Loftus)

"Not infrequently, the *a* in my 1928 portable has a mind of its own (aided and abetted by its keyboard position and an insufficiently powerful little finger – sinister, no doubt!), and provides an unexpected and unwanted space. When 'notable' emerged as 'not able,' I thought of the exercise of discovering opposites through the mere insertion of a space. The only other one I thought of, but not a very commendable example, is pro life ration.

Perhaps this country's range of longitude could produce a display of latitude through long etude." (L.E. Jones)

WHERE'S MY PRIZE?

Occasionally, I admit, the Challenge machinery grinds slowly. The winner of each week's contest is entitled to a book, and I send the prizes out, with the help and forbearance of Suzanne Buhasz, every four or five weeks. At least, I do so if I remember. Sometimes I can't find an address, or can't remember when I last sent books out, and I move on to other things. Then the letters drift in from winners curious to know whatever happened to that book they were promised two months earlier.

From John Lewis Watson, addressed to the Mope & Wail: "Dear sir: I wun 1st prize in yer Life on Mars compition and I ain't seen nuttin' of my reward as promised. What's with yous guys??!!! I wuz partickerly angshus to get the G&M Style Book. Sinse I only went to the School of Hard Nox (Upper Canada College), I ain't had much chance fer bein eddictated like yous gernalists and I figgered the book would improve by style, if necessary. Please forward, like yesterday, huh?"

From Bill Plumb, on February 1, 2000: "I do believe in you – I really do! But it's so hard for me to believe that there really is a Globe and Mail Style Book. Please, Santa, help me believe! Your little friend, Virginia."

From Al Wilkinson: "So far the highly anticipated book has not arrived. Did I win in a week when no prize was awarded? Did it go astray in the mail? Did one of your mailroom employees keep it as *part of an ambitious self-study program aimed at promotion to editor? Is the style book out of print? Did you decide that I'm already too stylish? Are there enough alternatives to form the subject of a Challenge?"*

Fortunately, the books do reach everyone who has won one, though sometimes they surprise the recipients. "I didn't realize I rated a gift (besides the accolades from my friends)," Irene Hobsbawn wrote back.

And sometimes – well, sometimes I have to wonder whether I should be doing more. From George Hrischenko, in a self-review of a Challenge entry he sent in 1998: "This is so good that when you fall off your chair in hysterics you will send me two *prize books."*

INDEX OF CONTRIBUTORS

·